He Did What?

True Stories of Resilient Women
Who Rose Above Betrayal and
How You Can, Too

Emily Collins

Table of Contents

Introduction

Lora Cheadle was an attorney, a loving mom, and considered herself a devoted wife. She had recently turned 44, and found her love for her own body and in Burlesque dancing—a pursuit she thought her husband supported because he always came to all her shows. The family was just about to celebrate her youngest son's graduation from college too. But none of those happy things cushioned the blow of finding out that the man she loved and trusted most intimately had been having an affair over the last 15 years! What was worse was she had considered their marriage of 23 years solid and dependable. She had always considered herself lucky that she and her husband were able to work through their problems, providing a stable and happy environment for their kids. To find out how wrong she had been about everything was just the tip of the iceberg. She could not bring herself to fully understand or deal with the aftermath. When she confronted her husband he defensively blamed his choices on her—Lora's emotional "unavailability," attachment to the kids, love for Burlesque—everything about her, it seemed, was a problem.

Having always prided herself on being a trustworthy person, she had blindly thought that others would reciprocate similarly. The whole ordeal shattered her self-confidence. It dawned on her that her family life and the values she had held so dear had been a sham. It seemed unbelievable that she had been so blindly stupid as not to have realized sooner.

Eventually, when faced with two more instances of his affairs, she could not bear it. She talked to her husband, if only to understand why he had done this. This time, he broke down and revealed it was (and always had been) his fault. He was insecure about many things from his past—things Lora had no idea of. For the first time, she learned of his childhood with narcissistic parents. He admitted he was "sick" and needed help. She agreed to couple's therapy with her husband. She wanted to understand what had happened, but more importantly, come to terms with the truth that she did not deserve what he had done. She also saw that the onus of his betrayal was totally on him. She realized that she could not have done anything any differently to have prevented her husband from cheating on her.

With these insights in place, Lora Cheadle turned her life around. She separated from her husband, giving him the space to work on his life and deal with his past trauma. Meanwhile, she did not sit around waiting for him. She is a TEDx speaker, podcaster, and an award-winning author of the self-help book *Flaunt! Drop Your Cover and Reveal Your Smart, Sexy, & Spiritual Self.*

When her husband returned a few years later, showing up for her and their marriage, Lora accepted him back into her life. She, however, makes it amply clear today that as much as she is committed to giving her marriage another chance, she expects her husband to do his work, be fully transparent with her, and be committed to their relationship (Cheadle, 2023).

Dear reader, if you have picked up this book, then you may have gone through an episode similar to that of Lora. You may have experienced hurt, betrayal, abuse, or trauma from the actions of a person you loved and trusted. You might be reeling from confusion, anger, fear, frustration, hurt, feeling stupid or vulnerable.

Fears of getting hurt again may hold you back from living a full life. The guilt of not having tried enough, may torment you and affect your daily actions and decisions. You might feel angry with the person who betrayed you and may unconsciously transfer some of that anger onto yourself for not having been wiser or bolder before. You may also feel trapped in recurrent thoughts and feelings.

If you identify with some or most of what I describe above, then you have picked up the right resource. *He Did What? True Stories of Resilient Women Who Rose Above Betrayal and How You Can, Too* is a unique book that aims to collect and collate stories of diverse women who have experienced the worst kinds of heartbreak. These women survived to tell their stories so that we can learn from their example in picking up the pieces of our lives. These kind, tough, remarkable women have rebuilt their lives brick by brick and achieved success in rewriting their stories.

If there is one constant we can take away from their lives, it is that betrayal does not end the victim's life. Even in the hardest of situations, it is possible to rise, withstand pressure, surmount obstacles, fight back, and lay a new foundation for one's life. This book can give you vital clues in helping with each kind of hurdle you may face because a sister somewhere has already tackled it before you and is willing to share her story with you.

Some of your questions it will answer include:

- Was it my fault? (NO!)

- What do I do now?

- Is it even possible to move on and live once more? (YES!)

- Can I find meaning, joy, and love again? (YES!)

- What if it happens again?

What sets this book apart from others is that it relies on human psychology without delving into the science of it in boring detail. It talks of the human condition and philosophizes without preaching. It covers stories of women of different ages, who are from different backgrounds and ethnicities so that every reader has at least one story with which they can strongly relate to.

And yet, this book is not a storybook. It weaves in practical and actionable strategies for overcoming pain and heartache and finding meaning, joy, and hope in life. Ultimately, this book aims to inspire and inform you about all the wonderful options and opportunities that lie ahead of you.

Chapter 1:

Channeling Anger Right

Anybody can become angry-that is easy; but to be angry with the right person, and to the right degree, and at the right time, and for the right purpose, and in the right way-that is not within everybody's power and is not easy.
—Aristotle

Her therapist narrates Daisy's story in a moving blog post, after a brief disclaimer that Daisy's real name and identity have been protected at her request. Daisy was a 19-year-old virgin when she met her high school sweetheart, whom she went on to marry. Though modern in her outlook, she was old-school in wanting her first time with the love of her life to be great. She saved herself for the "right man."

After the marriage, things started going downhill. Her husband seemed not to be interested in her physically and could hardly maintain his erection with her. She, on the other hand, fantasized about having a vigorous physical relationship with him. After all, that is what popular culture often tells us about young love. Unfortunately, this torrid physical relationship never materialized for Daisy. She grappled with thoughts of not being attractive enough for her husband, not being good enough in bed, and so on.

Daisy decided to "fix" the lack of intimacy between her and her husband. She spent money on lingerie and sex toys, organized special romantic weekends away, and even altered her appearance by getting herself breast implants to become sexier for her husband. However, these things, which should have made her feel better, only decreased her self-esteem as she felt "pornified" and still had to beg for sex from her husband. She often cried herself to sleep and masturbated once he slept to meet her physical needs.

With time and experience, Daisy understood that she had nothing to do with her husband's odd behavior. For one thing, he was extremely sensitive and secretive about her handling his phone or computer. On the few occasions that she could access these, she found that his browsing history was meticulously erased every time.

Finally, she discovered that her husband was addicted to porn and that was why she got so little of him. Daisy's anger raged red. He had never once told her of his problem and even when she had tried to talk to him, he often gaslighted her, making her feel like she was the one to blame. She couldn't help but feel deeply upset that, despite having the choice of any man she wanted, she was stuck with one who didn't seem to care for her. Moreover, though in her prime, she felt that she was being deprived of her womanhood and youthfulness, with her husband's lack of physical interest in her for months together.

Initially, she and her husband tried to work on their marriage with some success. They even had a beautiful pair of twins, who brought joy into Daisy's life. However, eventually, her husband returned to his old ways, and Daisy knew that there was little she could do to change his addiction if he did not work on it. She had been lied to too often to have any faith in his words. She briefly spiraled downward in negativity and even engaged with other men inappropriately to get back some attention she knew she deserved in her marriage. She felt guilty and embarrassed after these moments because she knew she was only losing her self-esteem in these pursuits.

Daisy's greatest strength in all her tribulations was her unerring self-perception. With the help of her therapist, Daisy tried to channel her anger, not at her husband alone, but at picking herself up. She rebuilt her confidence, life, and hobbies and recouped a little at a time.

Today, she is more at ease with herself. She regained the upper hand in her relationship with her husband because she learned to draw her boundaries. He knows that if he continues cheating, manipulating, and gaslighting her, Daisy will be forced to leave. She has learned to put the safety, security, and sanity of herself and her kids before that of her husband. In her therapist's words, Daisy has become "a force to reckon with" (stimothybrown, 2019).

Converting Bitterness to Rightful Anger

Daisy's story is familiar in its heart-rending aspect of women who always think they are to blame for the problems in their romantic relationships. The lengths to which Daisy went in "fixing" the issues were always targeted at herself. She tried to change her appearance and attitude to become more desirable to her husband. Ironically, it was not until she found her own voice and power that her husband started respecting her!

Anger has its place in human emotions and can be as powerful as it is destructive. Anger is not a negative emotion, as we often are taught to believe. In fact, like joy or excitement, anger is also a normal human reaction to situations and people that let us down. Anger allows us to see that we have been wronged.

A lack of anger often signals a lack of self-respect. For instance, when somebody puts you down, hurts, or cheats you, it is only natural to feel angry. When you don't feel or express your anger, this might give the message that you don't mind being taken advantage of.

When anger is left untreated, unaddressed, or unexpressed, it can turn into bitterness and resentment. In Daisy's example, her realization of her husband's condition made her rightfully angry. As a wife, she was indignant as to why he had never let her in on his issue. So far, so good for Daisy, because she was suddenly learning to question the person who had been taking her love for him for granted.

However, when she used that same anger in trying to forge brief relationships with other men, it did not give her the power or self-respect that she dearly craved. On the contrary, she felt she was cheapening herself further. Daisy's bitterness turned inward upon herself, something she quickly learned was not doing her or her relationship any favors.

In short, it is not your anger that is at fault. Anger is perfectly alright as long as you know what to do with it and how to employ it for your growth.

Channeling Anger Right

Being trapped in anger can lead to several negative consequences such as bitterness, frustration, recurring and unresolved fights and arguments with your partner, and worst of all, a lack of care for yourself and the way you are treated.

So what do you do if you feel incredibly angry?

Step One: Hold On

Anger can make people hasty in their decisions. It clouds your better judgment, making you do, say, or act in ways you wouldn't generally want to behave. This is why, things said or done in anger invariably leave us feeling regretful, ashamed, or guilty later on.

Therefore, hold on. When you know you are angry, acknowledge how you feel. Admit why and with whom you feel angry. Your feelings are valid. However, do not act on your anger just yet. Hold on for a while until you feel calmer. Obviously, you cannot expect yourself to feel at peace, but at least you can wait until you feel you have a grip on yourself and your next action.

Step Two: Manage Yourself

Do what it takes to manage your emotions. Don't worry too much about how to handle the other person. You neither have to engage and argue with them, nor do you have to soothe and make them feel better. This moment is for you. Breathe deeply, engage in things that bring you joy, work if that helps, or just relax and take time off.

This step is the key to mastering your own feelings and freedom. You are not running away from your emotions or the situation. You are merely rallying your thoughts and energies and putting them where they count, leading to productive solutions. Only when you feel you are ready to face your partner's betrayal, you will confront them.

Step Three: Communicate

So often, betrayal spawns all the releases the worst parts of ourselves. We feel vindicated in deliberately trying to hurt our partner. We feel justified in "hitting back" at them because they are the ones who cheated us. However, this tit-for-tat policy, though perhaps bringing short-term gratification, provides no long-term solution, happiness, or peace.

It's in your best interest to speak openly and honestly about why their actions hurt you. Be clear about why you feel betrayed and why you can never trust them. In turn, give them a chance to explain and listen to their version of things. You don't have to agree with everything they say, but fairness demands that you give them an ear. Once they are done speaking, you can express what aspects you disagree with. Focus on building a logical flow of arguments.

While communicating, ensure you don't get defensive or shut yourself down. Defensive behavior will get picked on and could lead to further fights. Shutting down will not give you any closure, and will prevent your own healing.

Step Four: Avoid Triangles

A subtext of communication, this draws upon Daisy's story. When we are angry with our partners, we often feel tempted to involve a friend or family member. Convenient and gratifying as this might feel, avoid this entirely. When you bring another person into the equation, you stand to lose sight of what you really want. The person may sway you in your judgment of yourself and your partner. It can also breed unnecessary jealousy.

If you feel the need to involve another person, let it be a marriage therapist or counselor who will listen to both sides of the problem neutrally, before giving you their views.

In a later chapter of this book, we will discuss situations in which you may have to confide in a trusted person outside your relationship.

However, as a general maxim, the more is not the merrier where a marital or romantic relationship is concerned.

Step Five: Decision Time and Recognizing Your Worth

After you and your partner have spent time discussing the problem from all angles, comes the crucial time to decide—what next? Now is the time to contemplate who your partner is. Some questions you can ask yourself now are:

- What do I feel for my partner?

- Do I still love them?

- Is my partner capable of change?

- If they show signs of changing, how much time should I give them to work on themselves and our relationship?

- If they aren't capable of change, what can I do? Should I stick it out or leave?

- What would be the repercussions of my decision (whether I decide to stay or not) on my kids, extended family, finances, etc.?

This part is something that, eventually, you must decide for yourself. Therapy or an external agent can guide you through the process, but should not make the decision for you. It is your choice entirely whether to move on or stay in the relationship.

However, whatever your final decision, it should come with a de facto principle for yourself: I will not compromise my happiness, health, and mental peace in any situation. I deserve to be loved and cherished in my relationship, and have no obligation to put up with things where my needs aren't being met.

Chapter 2:

Reclaiming "Faith"—

Whatever It Means to You

She is clothed with strength and dignity, and she laughs without fear of the future.
—Proverbs 31:25-31

Stacey Szczepanski has been a teacher for 14 years and an ardent believer in God's love. A traveler and ambivert, Stacey had no idea what she was setting herself up for when she decided to try out online dating. Coming from a wonderfully loving, faithful family, Stacey's ideas about evil and wickedness were rather vague, perhaps. She admits today she was naive and trusting. Moreover, her online match, "Dave," was handsome, claimed to own a house, said all the right things during their calls, and even shared plenty of pictures from his life with her.

Stacey blindly fell into this fairytale trap. Stacey had moved cities once and continued seeing other people, but Dave was a constant in her life. By the time when Stacey "committed" to him, she had "known" Dave for nearly seven years! Things had even come to the point where she was planning to move to California—to be with him. However, the relationship was not without its downs. She had never yet met him. Dave often manipulated and gaslighted her. Over time, things he said did not make sense to her. Her friends warned her that his disinclination to meet her after all this time, seemed a huge red flag and that she should hire a private investigator to keep tabs on him. She was often left feeling confused and tired after her conversations with him. The once vibrant and joyful woman was slowly turning inward, to such an extent that her parents were getting extremely worried.

She finally decided to investigate the matter on her own. Stacey used to watch the MTV program *Catfish* earlier and decided to take a cue from the show and do an online search with her "boyfriend's" photos. To her horror, she found pictures of Dave all over the internet, but just that it was not him. The photos were of a man named Andrew Canter, an architect in California, with a fiancée named Ariana! Stacey felt numb with shock when she realized that she had been revealing the most intimate parts of her life with a complete stranger and his circle of friends, who all turned out to be fraudsters behind fake profiles!

Stacey took hold of her life even though inwardly she was crumbling. She slowly rebuilt herself. She got back to work, renewed her faith in Jesus, and started traveling widely. Eventually, she also found the courage and peace to write the book *Unlocking Love: How Being Catfished Deepened My Faith and Led Me on a Journey to Wholeness* (2023). She has given her story her voice in the audiobook version, and multiple interviews about her story and her healing journey. She is meanwhile enjoying her gift of singleness and living her life to the fullest (Szczepanski, 2024 & Szczepanski, 2023).

Watch Out for "Too Good to be True"

Stacey tells us time and again that you should be wary of people who seem "too good to be true," especially when you meet them behind technology. In her interviews, she says that people who generally seem extremely sincere, charming, and great are in real life anything but those.

Despite her humiliation, Stacey decided to go public with her story, because she feels online cheating like catfishing isn't addressed enough. There are thousands of women like her, who get manipulated and tricked by sweet-talking crooks, who claim that they will give them a life. Unfortunately, these characters use fake profiles and pictures to create a persona that does not exist.

We may often think that the pain these deceived women experience is not as bad as loving and losing a person in the flesh, because, after all, they did not "meet" their predators. However, we would be doing them a grave injustice by not acknowledging their heartache. These are women who invested their time, energy, and sometimes even their hard-earned money into a relationship they believed was rooted in love and trust. Having to lose the relationship, and realize that it was all a smokescreen, is perhaps even more terrible a plight than a cheating partner or spouse.

Catfishing is a form of cyberbullying where someone pretends to be a friend or confidant online, manipulating and deceiving you through mind games. Catfishing is not just always financial fraud, but also emotionally using the victim by luring them into a fake relationship. Catfishers use a person's deepest and darkest secrets or vulnerabilities against them. When a victim gives them information about themselves trustingly, the catfisher uses it to gain an upper hand over them, often even blackmailing them with that information.

As Stacey tells us, there is no single reason why a catfisher does the evil that they do. It could be a way for them to cope with their own insecurities or a form of mental illness. Some people get a thrill from trolling and hurting others—things they can't do in their own names. So, they steal another's identity and hide behind a screen to vent their frustrations. Some online bullies think that catfishing is a great way of taking revenge against a person who has let them down. Some do it to a total stranger to experiment with their own sexualities. Some others win the trust of their victims to eventually con them out of money. Whatever, their reasons are, we can agree that catfishing is one of the biggest dangers the modern world faces.

There is only one real remedy against online harassment—being wary of people and exercising your discretion when it comes to forming an opinion about people online. Watch out in particular for people who:

- Love bomb: Remember that they may have spent time intently studying your online presence. They will say the right things, making you feel like you'll have a lot in common. They will claim to have the same hobbies and interests as you. They will also keep praising you about your looks, personality, or wit to make you feel "heard and seen."

- Rush you into relationships: Catfishers often act fast in forming a relationship with you. They'll seek to capture your full attention and manipulate you to achieve that goal.

- Seem to have too few other followers or friends: One tell-tale sign of a fake account will be a lack of many followers or friends.

- Avoid meeting or calling you in person: Be cautious about people who avoid meeting or calling you in real-time. These are people who have a lot to hide.

- Tell you tales that are too exciting or don't add up: Keep track of what they are doing because in all the lies they spin, at times, they might slip up and let out inconsistencies. Also, beware of people who claim to lead super-exciting lives all the time. Life can't be "happening" all the time, not even for celebrities!

- Ask you for money, sensitive information, or photos: Many catfishers work on you with an agenda. They may ask you for sensitive information like passwords, security equations, etc. on your accounts or for inappropriate photos or videos of yourself which they will use to blackmail you. Some others may ask you for money, using personal stories and cooked-up tragedies to gain your emotional sympathy.

- Upload or send you photos that look too professional or odd: Normal accounts will generally have photos taken by friends and families—many of them could be candid or not-so-perfect shots of the person. However, catfishers use professional-looking photos available on the web. They will crop out or not have other people and places around the person being shown. They may also never send you a real-time selfie of themselves. You can use Google Lens feature to find out if the photos being used are genuine ones or those that are downloaded from other profiles or sites.

In a nutshell, when dealing with a potential online date, ask yourself at all times, *Who are they really? What do they want from me?* Even so, the most careful among us can fall prey to these confidence tricksters. What then?

- **Gather evidence:** Keep records and screenshots of the messages, emails, and posts you have received from the fake account with time and date stamps. The more evidence you have, the easier it becomes to find, catch, and convict the scammer.

- **Block and report:** Use the block and report feature available on social networking websites to block and report fake profiles. This is always the first step in saving yourself from further harm when you recognize a scammer. You should also immediately change passwords or other security details of social or banking accounts you may have shared with this person in the past.

- **Contact the right authorities:** Apart from the report feature on the website, you can also contact the local cybercrime division in your city to lodge a complaint against such individuals. Your timely action could save the next victim from a similar plight.

We have discussed all that you can do physically against a catfisher. However, you may also need to undo the emotional damage that such a person wreaks upon you.

Finding Faith, Your Voice, and Healing

As with Stacey, broken trust could take a long time to salvage and repair. When you understand you were conned once, you might lose your faith in humanity itself—it could be a serious blow to your happiness and well-being. Finding your faith starts with reconnecting with yourself. Unless you believe you are worthy of being respected, loved, and cherished, it will prove an uphill task to connect with others again.

Stacey says she found God and religion to help her through her toughest times. However, you don't even have to be religious to have faith. It is only a matter of turning your story around to believe firmly that you did nothing wrong. In fact, somebody preyed on your kindness and ability to give love. This does not make you any less of a person.

Many victims often fear sharing their stories for being thought of as "fools", or worse, "enablers" who let their abusers get away with it. However, you can tell your story at your own time and pace, not just to prove that such a scenario could happen to anybody, but also to find healing. Writing or expressing your version helps you let go of some of that pain you may be unconsciously holding on to. Your story may also help other victims who have undergone or are undergoing a similar fate in recognizing patterns and saving themselves from further hurt.

Ultimately, every one of us needs a purpose that defines our happiness. You are the best judge of what your purpose is—God, religion, helping others, or any other pursuit that brings you love and fulfillment.

Chapter 3:

A Second Chance

You did what you knew how to do, and when you knew better, you did better.
—Maya Angelou

A woman who wishes her name not to be revealed tells us her moving story in a blog post in Oprah Winfrey's magazine. In the article, she reminisces back to a time when she was a mistress of a married man. She was in her early 30s and fed up with men who did not want to commit. The affair lasted only half a year, much of which she spent worrying about his wife. She was grateful to have met her warm, kind, and funny husband, Sam, who helped her end the unhealthy relationship with the married man.

This woman was no stranger to the fact that an affair was only a make-believe—a little time you spent with a person, in which passions ruled, and you could be as witty and romantic as you like. In her case, she could afford to overlook the irritating foibles of her partner because those were his wife's cross to bear, not hers.

Even so, it was devastating when Sam came home one evening and sat her down on the sofa, only a couple of months after they had moved to a new city, to tell her about his infidelity. He told her that the affair had been happening for three years. Despite her anger, she saw that the admission pained her husband, too—his face was crumpled and ashen with the magnitude of what he had done. He also told her he had ended it and wanted to prioritize her and their three small kids. Yet, he went on to explain that he had fallen in love with his colleague, with whom he worked on a long-term project.

The narrator tells us how this admission upended her life. She could not eat more than an egg and a piece of chocolate for months afterward. She barely caught more than two hours of sleep daily, and she occasionally hurt herself with a knife. She couldn't help digging through his laptop and even cut up a few of his sweaters and shirts. She woke him up at night to scream, swear, and sob at him. There was only one thing she knew at the time—she was not prepared for a divorce. She loved her husband, and she also had her kids to think about.

She also knew that fixing this marriage needed her work as much as his. She went for therapy, as did he. She realized that he was genuinely sorry for what he had done and even as she shouted at him, he took it quietly, all the while reiterating his heartfelt apology. He was even honest about all the details she wanted to know. He made it clear that he was going to take full responsibility for his actions and work on it so that such a breach of trust would never taint their relationship again.

It wasn't all rosy of course, and even till the end of the article the narrator is not sure how long it will take for her to get over this chapter, but she gains the profound wisdom that she would rather choose this bumpy uncertain path before her with her husband rather than without him (Anonymous, 2010).

Trusting Vs Taking for Granted

The story above seems to paint Sam in a poor light, until you reach the part where the narrator explains why she feels culpable, to an extent, for the deterioration of her marriage. She tells us that while she takes absolutely no blame for Sam's infidelity, which is his own burden to bear, over the twelve years of knowing him, she had begun to let go, ever so slightly, of the goodness in her marriage, instead focusing on the irritations within it. None of these ever escalated into a full-blown fight, but she admits that "a mild scorn and a habitual bitterness" had settled upon her whenever she dealt with her husband. What she had not known was that Sam too was grappling with his frustration with her slightly avoidant attitude.

On top of this, she was so confident about Sam's faithfulness to her that she felt she had probably taken him for granted. In all the years she had been married to him, it had never once occurred to her that he might or could cheat on her. Even though she wrote this off as absolute faith in him—a wonderful thing to have in your spouse—at the back of her mind, she knew she had also failed to give him his due. In admitting this, she is in no way condoning his adultery.

There is a fine line between trust and taking for granted, especially in intimate relationships. When this line is crossed, partners begin to observe each other only in the light of the mundane expectations they have of each other. This can lead to a decline of not just passion, but also warmth. Even loving relationships can thus be eroded of affection over time.

In conclusion, there are two things you must proactively do within your relationship:

- As much as you condemn your partner's choice to stray (that's totally on them, not you) be wary of opportunities where you can make better choices in your relationship.

- Secondly, give credit where it is due. Notice and appreciate their efforts and willingness to do the work in repairing the relationship if they are doing it.

Where Remorse Is Genuine:

Relationships Outliving Infidelity

How can we ever know if our partner, who may have been unfaithful once, will be faithful henceforth? How can we ensure that infidelity will never happen again? Unfortunately, there is no magic potion or wand which can conclusively make these happen for you.

What we can do is only take a few cautionary steps and then hope that our partner promises to keep their side of the bargain. No! This does not mean that you should close your eyes to their indiscretions indefinitely or that you should give them a second chance. After all, it is your relationship, for you to choose how it must proceed.

The following are only some guidelines you may use in your journey forward:

- **Follow your gut:** Often, you can gauge the genuineness of someone promising you loyalty. You can use your past experience as a framework against which to decide whether they mean what they say or not. Sometimes, you know in the pit of your stomach that they don't mean what they say. Whether you choose to stay in your relationship or not, do not ignore what your instinct tells you. You don't have to act rashly on your instinct by getting into frequent fights and arguments. You can merely take note of what your gut is trying to tell you. This will help you remain cautiously optimistic in your journey after a heartbreak. This way, you will be giving your partnership another chance, but with the directive in stone that you will no longer tolerate being fooled.

- **There is a way ahead:** Having made the previous point, open your heart to the knowledge that infidelity is not the end of the road. Stop dwelling on it as if you have done something wrong to deserve to be cheated on. If it has happened, and if you intend to move past it, then you need to look at the positives in your relationship. Think of all the reasons why you still want to be with your partner and how you'll make a complementary couple, mature enough to look ahead into a bright future. Think about the lessons you learned from the episode and what you would like to change in your relationship going forth. Again, the mandatory proviso here will be that you require them to be fully honest and open with you.

- **Be (brutally and kindly) honest:** Relationships, even the best of ones, are a lot of work. One of the most important things that strengthens a relationship is honesty. There is a misconception that honesty can't coexist with kindness. However, this is far from the truth. Be brutally honest with yourself and with your partner. You can express the truth (as you see it) politely and softly, but firmly too. Ask yourself and them questions that matter, and don't shy away from difficult conversations. Also remember, your truth may not always be their truth. When conflicts arise, they may feel as justified in behaving the way they did, as you did in feeling hurt. This is why open, frequent, and quality communication is so vital.

- **Give and take space:** Relationships after infidelity can be exhausting. You may love the person who cheated on you and be confused about why you are staying back. At the same time, if they made a one-time mistake, you may genuinely feel pity for them. It can be a tumultuous time as they decide how to work on mending the damage done, and as you chart out a plan of action on how to proceed. During this time, it is essential that both partners should come together to discuss and resolve their conflicts. It is also important for both people to take time out for themselves to understand where they stand and what they want out of the relationship. You should know what you need personally and for the security of your relationship.

- **Relationships might be strengthened by affairs:** Dr. Peggy Vaughan, an advocate for open communication in marriage, is known for her book, *The Monogamy Myth: A Personal Handbook for Recovering from Affairs* (2009). She found in her research that couples who openly discuss infidelity and work through it can sometimes experience stronger emotional intimacy afterward, though this is not the norm. In her work, Vaughan notes that many couples who survive infidelity and work to rebuild their relationship do so through significant effort, mutual commitment, and often with the help of therapy. Research backs the fact that some relationships become stronger because one of the partners strayed. One incident like that might force both individuals to take a closer look at what was missing in their equation and work on the problems. This is not to say that infidelity is mandatory for a stronger relationship. This statement does not excuse infidelity, either. However, should you decide to stay put, it can provide hope in the revival of your relationship.

Ultimately, find the grace in choosing whatever you think is right for you. Remember, there is only one of you and life is too short to throw away on regrets.

Chapter 4:

Closure in Using

Empowering Language

Someday you're gonna look back on this moment of your life as such a sweet time of grieving. You'll see that you were in mourning and your heart was broken, but your life was changing...
—Elizabeth Gilbert

Vi was distraught. It was her father's funeral, and she was face to face with the husband she had left behind some 25 years ago. This man had abused her physically and emotionally, and had also been a womanizer. Vi's parents, however, had chosen to support her ex-husband through the nasty and humiliating court case in which there were charges against him for violence. Now, years later, here was the man in front of her in the flesh, sitting calmly with the woman with whom he had cheated when still married to Vi.

To her horror, the ex-husband was not only one of the pallbearers, but also the one reading the eulogy. Vi could feel eyes boring into her as he got up to speak about her late father's life. At the graveside, Vi comforted her mother and was walking away, when he caught up with her, hugged her, and kissed her on the lips, remarking how happy he was to see her. She had no choice and stood by as she realized they were being photographed.

Vi had no intention of backing down. She stood her ground, and looked at the man who had shredded her confidence, destroyed the relationship with her family, and caused her extreme pain, in his eyes. And then, miraculously, magically, she found the words she had only recently practiced in her drama therapy workshop. She could utter them calmly and coherently: "You betrayed me, our love, and the only request I had made of our relationship". The lines were borrowed from a play based on the African Folk Tale "The Woman From the Stars," but they did the trick.

To onlookers, it might have seemed like she was simply exchanging pleasantries with her ex-husband, but she knew in her heart that her healing was complete. This man, a wealthy and prominent businessman of the community, had driven a wedge between her family and her. After their separation, he had left her with no choice but to run away from her home, and take solace and a job in the city. But thankfully for Vi, she had also rediscovered the power of her words. She knew she was in absolute control of her voice and what she needed to say (Vi & Schrader, 2022).

Using Empowering Words

Like Vi, you may perhaps be still grappling with the aftermath of what happened. You, too, may be searching for the words that will bring closure and healing. However, don't give up hope. It is only a matter of finding the right words and using them in the right situation.

Words have a potent way of bringing healing and hope. They can change the course of your actions and even make you feel invincible. Lao Tzu once said, "Watch your thoughts, they become your words; watch your words, they become your actions; watch your actions, they become your habits; watch your habits, they become your character; watch your character, it becomes your destiny" (Johnson, 2021).

Something as simple as choosing the words in our heads and the ones that leave our mouths can make a huge impact on our journey ahead. There is no general template that anyone can create for these words, for they must resonate with you and make you feel powerful. You need to be intentional while choosing them.

One of the most powerful ways of finding the right words could be to write a letter to the person who betrayed your trust. This letter is for your eyes alone—you don't have to send it to them, but you can perfect this letter, adding to it as your healing journey progresses. Be aware of the repercussions of your words. There are things that you may say in the heat of the moment but may regret in the long run. This is why you should take your time over this letter. As far as possible, refrain from cursing or using profanity. Similarly, avoid pettiness. Instead, focus on how they have hurt you and in what ways they betrayed your trust. Make it clear, simple, and a powerful testament to your feelings.

Dear _____,

This letter isn't for you; it's for me. After everything that's happened, I've finally found my voice. You broke my trust, my heart, and left scars I didn't deserve. But I won't carry that pain any longer.

I've spent too much time blaming you and wondering why. Now, I see this isn't about fault. It's about choices. You made yours, and I made mine.

What you did hurt me deeply, but I've chosen peace. I'm releasing the weight of betrayal because my story doesn't end here—it only begins. I'm learning to love and value myself in ways I didn't before. Your actions won't define me.

I've realized that I deserve honesty, respect, and love without conditions. You couldn't give me that, and that's okay. I won't seek closure in your words or actions anymore. My closure is in the growth I've embraced.

I hope you find what you're looking for, but I won't be part of that search. I'm moving forward, and in doing so, I'm finding peace.

Goodbye.

Sincerely,

_____

The above is only for an idea. You don't have to use the same words or style. The intent is for you to say calmly and clearly what you have been bottling up. The letter is to them, but ultimately, for your growth and peace. In this epistle you create, rewrite, and fine-tune, you might find a statement that resonates with you most. This is perhaps the key to your healing.

Next, you need to say it aloud to yourself imagining you are facing the person or people who broke you once. Ridiculous as this may seem at first, this role play could help you voice your deepest emotions. You can either use a mirror or simply imagine a scenario when you might have to face them.

Here is a letter I wrote long ago in the wake of something bad that happened to me. It was a letter I put myself into with all my heart. It says everything I want to and nothing unnecessarily negative. I encourage you to create your own letter of healing.

Ultimately, whether you get a chance to directly address the people who may have hurt you in the past or not, being prepared with the words in itself is a battle won. This whole process could be a gradual one, as you accustom yourself to voicing your real thoughts and opinions after years of having been forced to suppress them. Vi had the wonderful opportunity to find and practice her words aloud during her therapy. You, too, might need to find out how and where to master your words.

Letting Go

Vi found her closure in saying her words, succinctly but powerfully, to her abuser-betrayer. Not all of us may get the same opportunity. Sometimes, over time and a myriad of other situations, we may never find the chance to tell them how they made us feel. Sometimes, our words may lose their power over time or for whatever reason, and we may feel that it no longer makes sense to call or write to them. That's okay.

Your closure doesn't have to depend on them or their reaction to your words. Some people don't even deserve parting words from you.

Learning to walk away from such situations and people is also crucial. Stay away from people who don't intend to get better. Leave things behind that can't be changed. Be in control of things and people you wish to retain in your life—be mindful of why you want them and how they contribute to your wellness, happiness, and wholeness.

Some changes you can make for this to happen are:

- **Accept:** Accept and acknowledge that something bad happened to you, not because you did anything wrong, but because you were kind to a person who was unworthy of your trust and love. Acknowledge that there is nothing you can do to change what happened, but also remember the lesson the episode has taught you. Encourage yourself to see what happened merely as one page out of the big book of your life.

- **Release:** Actively seek ways to release all the fear, anger, frustration, and other pent-up emotions. Now is the time to seek therapy, a trusted person to talk to, or even the page of a notebook to scribble away your inner turmoil. Think, write, and speak until you feel your story is ready to be told. Of course, you can choose not to tell it too, that's also your prerogative.

- **Forgive:** You don't have to forgive the other person. If you can, that's wonderful. Whether they apologize or not, at times, you will need to find closure in yourself. It is also possible that their apology, after everything said and done, may bring you no additional peace. There is, however, one important step. You have to forgive yourself. Your healing is vitally dependent on you forgiving yourself. You can tell yourself as many times as it takes for you to believe it that you made no mistake, and are wiser for the choices you made. Tell yourself that your kindness is your greatest strength, even if somebody chose to use it against you.

- **Surrender:** Surrender is not inaction. It is so often linked to failure or defeat that this word is seen in a negative light. However, the surrender we talk of here is a complete acceptance of what is and faith in the process. You don't have to control things around you. You choose to watch and understand them first and take action in your best interests. You don't have to struggle or fight your emotions. You let them pass through you until they can no longer upset you.

Finally, embrace the journey of rediscovering your voice, and choose how to use it in a way that feels right for you. Whether you decide to speak with those who hurt you or quietly let go, let your choice come from a place of personal wisdom and inner peace. May each step reflect your growth and the strength you've found along the way.

Chapter 5:

Defining What Betrayal Means

to You

Every betrayal contains a perfect moment, a coin stamped heads or tails with salvation on the other side.
–Barbara Kingsolver

Six years down the lane, Ashlynn caught her husband having an emotional affair. He swore he had never cheated on her physically and she had no reason to doubt him either. But Ashlynn was devastated. She reflected on how her husband relied on porn to meet his physical needs, while another woman now fulfilled his emotional ones. Where did that leave her?—she wondered. She felt so alone and unhappy in her marriage.

The turning point came when she reconnected with a friend on Facebook. This woman, too, had recently divorced her cheating husband. For the first time, Ashlynn opened up about her husband's addiction. Her friend invited her to a conference on betrayal trauma, and everything made sense for Ashlynn. Suddenly, she could name the emotion she was feeling. She felt that her anger and hurt were valid, given her husband's actions.

Ashlynn always told her family she and her husband, Coby, had the "perfect marriage." However, even from year one of her marriage, she felt something wasn't right. Perhaps he did watch porn on the side, but she could never put a finger on it. He definitely seemed to hide a lot of things from her, and even the littlest mistakes often made her react terribly. On the whole, she was prone to dismiss everything as "something wrong" with herself.

Ashlynn and Coby signed up for therapy. He had his individual therapy too. One day, he came home from one of his sessions and confessed he had another affair. Ashlynn cried in the bathroom. It was just so hard. However, she also knew she wasn't ready to give up on him. She was willing to work with him if he was agreeable. Ashlynn learned more about her husband's addiction and actively helped him as he worked on repairing his relationship with her. Today, Ashlynn and Coby have just celebrated their 15th wedding anniversary. Ashlynn is glad she spent time trying to learn more about his problem and feels that it has paid off in the love and respect they now share. She also tells women like her that no matter how terrible it may seem, there is hope for a relationship after infidelity (Addo, 2018).

Identifying the Signs of an Emotional Affair

An emotional affair is when a partner turns away from his committed relationship to seek emotional support from another person. The partner may reveal things about his relationship and spouse to this outsider. This constitutes infidelity, even if the person cheating has not been sexually or physically intimate with the second person.

An emotional affair can be as bad or worse than a physical affair, because the person engaging in it steps on their relationship, neglects their partner, and instead of focusing on fixing things within the relationship has revealed intimate details to a stranger.

So, how can you identify the signs of an emotional affair? The following are some signals to such an affair.

- **The initial revelation:** Not every person sets out deliberately to have an affair or cheat on their partners. When they meet someone new they are attracted to, who pays them attention, they may talk about this new person to their partners in the superlative. The person they're probably spending more time with will be "good at their job", "incredibly kind", or "such a great listener." At this stage, a partner is perhaps only infatuated with this new person and doesn't mean to actively sabotage their marriage or relationship.

- **Secrecy:** As the partner is drawn more into the new relationship, they may spend more time on their phone or laptop and will be wary about their significant other handling their devices. This sudden secrecy is a tell-tale sign of something wrong. Secrecy always means that the person embarking on it knows they have crossed some line.

- **Distance:** Every couple develops occasional cold phases in their relationship. However, if this distance increases over the time that the partner makes a new acquaintance, then it is probably something to watch out for. As they get more comfortable opening up about their lives to this new individual, they will not have as much time or energy to spend with their committed partner. Slowly, the emotional distance between the partners will increase.

- **Lack of intimacy:** Even if a partner cheats "only" emotionally, they may still find that they are no longer interested in their significant other. They will make excuses to get out of intimacy and sex. There may also be incidents when the cheating partner finds fault with the other person or is unwarrantedly mean or critical of them, simply to vindicate their behavior. They may try to make it seem like the partners are responsible for them turning to another person.

- **Unusual behavior or changes in routine:** A partner who suddenly takes a new-found interest in grooming themselves or becoming fitness-conscious should not be a worrying sign under normal circumstances. Some people merely want a better lifestyle for themselves, and why should a loving partner stand in the way? However, sudden changes in dressing, or longer hours at work, etc. should raise one's antennae especially when coupled with some or all of the signs we have already discussed above.

Assume you have ascertained that someone you love is having an emotional affair, how do you handle this, especially when you may feel angry and hurt at the betrayal? This is what we will look at next.

Dealing With and Healing From an Emotional Affair

Dealing with emotional cheating can be incredibly challenging because it involves a betrayal of trust and intimacy, even if it doesn't involve a physical act of cheating. Here are some steps you can consider if you're faced with emotional cheating:

Acknowledge Your Feelings

Emotional cheating can evoke intense feelings like betrayal, sadness, and anger. It's important to acknowledge and validate your emotions. As with any loss, allow yourself to grieve. You have the right to treat emotional cheating as a significant breach of trust and give yourself permission to process the pain.

Sometimes, feeling the pain brings greater healing than numbing oneself to it. World-renowned researcher and professor, Brené Brown, says that inuring yourself to pain and sadness will also result in you numbing yourself to the good feelings of joy and love (Brown & TED, 2011). In other words, over time your capacity to humanly feel things will reduce, giving rise to frustration and restlessness. Therefore, permit yourself to feel the pain, and slowly, heal yourself through it.

Take time for yourself because emotional cheating can take a toll on your mental health. Prioritize self-care, and ensure you have a support system, like trusted family or friends, to lean on during the time.

Reinvest in Yourself

Hanging onto a relationship in which you feel you have no place can indeed take a huge toll on your confidence and self-esteem. You are bound to ask yourself things like *Am I not good enough? Why was I not enough?* and so on. Though these thoughts are normal enough, pandering on them excessively can do you no good. They will only drag you down further into the mire.

Reaffirm your self-worth and remember that emotional cheating is not a reflection of your worth. Keep your confidence and self-esteem intact. Every infidelity has a moment of choice where the cheating person had a choice. If your partner chose to turn their back on the relationship they shared with you, that's on them.

Do whatever it takes to feel good about yourself. This may look different for different individuals. Some may want to exercise more, while others may want to spend more time pursuing mindful living or meditation. One may find joy in grooming themselves and trying out new styles, while another may want to spend more time on hobbies they love. Whatever gives you joy, accept it wholeheartedly, without judgment. You deserve to feel whole again.

Communicate Honestly

Will your partner get it, own it, and fix it? These are the questions that you need answered next. Confront the issue and prepare to have an open, honest conversation with your partner. Calmly express how their emotional connection with someone else makes you feel, and ask them to clarify their actions.

If you can, avoid accusations, though I admit that's easier said than done. Accusations generally provide no results because the person who cheated on you deliberately won't be moved by it, and a person who unwittingly got into it will only get defensive.

Instead, if you can focus on expressing how their behavior impacts you emotionally, it might get both of you ahead.

Assess the Relationship

Evaluate the state of your relationship and reflect on whether your emotional needs are being met and whether your partner feels similarly.

Often emotional cheating doesn't happen in a vacuum. It often occurs when one partner feels emotionally disconnected or unfulfilled. This is, again, not to say that you are at fault, for not having given enough to your partner, but understanding the underlying reasons for their infidelity could give you a better perspective on why it happened and help you prevent it from happening in the future.

Set Boundaries

Express your intentions without holding them over yourself and your partner, especially if you choose to stay in the relationship. This step is crucial going ahead. You must define what you consider emotional cheating. Since each relationship is different, it may take some effort to make your partner realize that their actions are harming the foundation of your bonding. You can clarify what kinds of emotional intimacy you find inappropriate for your partner to have with another person, and how you'd like both of you to interact with others.

If you mean to repair the relationship from its roots, mutually agreeing on boundaries is key. The boundaries you set must be those both you and your partner can respect, and that can ensure the comfort of both moving forward.

Seek Support

Talk to a therapist. A third party's unbiased and professional perspective can help you navigate the situation and your emotions more clearly.

You can also consider couple therapy if you and your partner would like to work on the issues together. A therapist, with their expert knowledge and experience, can help foster better communication and healing, where partners are committed to the relationship.

Decide the Next Step

Even if both of you are willing to work through the situation, rebuilding trust takes time and effort, because both of you must be dedicated to improving the emotional connection. As we have seen from Ashlynn's story, though challenging, it is not as impossible as one would imagine.

On the other hand, if the emotional cheating is part of a larger pattern of similar abuse, or you feel you can't move forward, it might be time to reevaluate whether staying in the relationship is healthy or worth your time and effort.

Finally, understand there is no right approach to dealing with emotional infidelity. You must decide what feels right for you and move ahead in the supreme confidence that no matter what, you will not let yourself down.

Chapter 6:

Finding Peace After Betraying

That's the thing with betrayal- it's always the people you love.
—Fatima Bhutto

Samantha's is a slightly different story. She reached a crisis in her life, though seeming to have a perfect life and three great teenagers, whom she shared with her husband. Her husband, despite his occasional dalliances, gave the kids a secure life, and she had always shared a big intellectual bond with him. This is why she would never have imagined what would happen next.

For years, she had known David and his wife. They were family friends and often caught up with each other. David, like her, had grown-up children, another tie that deepened their friendship. Samantha and David had always shared a slight, mutual attraction but managed to keep it well under check. That was, until the day it happened. Samantha's husband had moved to London, where she and the kids were planning to join him soon. After a fundraiser, David and she were casually spending some time at an old western bar, where they danced together. They exchanged a few words. But somewhere Samantha knew a line had been crossed. The words they said to each other were perfectly true, and could not be unsaid. Samantha knew she had fallen irrevocably in love with David.

Samantha and David tried hard to keep away from each other, but it did not work—the pull between them was too strong. They debated telling their spouses and were aware of the terrible hurt it would bring to their families. And yet, there was also the missed happiness they had to consider if they did not tell their spouses.

When Samantha finally joined her husband in London, he asked her out of the blue if there was someone else. She had no option but to tell him the truth of her deception over the last four months. Meanwhile,

David told his wife, too. And thus started what was to become the first of several visits to Samantha's psychologist. Though she tried to be fair to her husband, she was sure that her life belonged with David. The only thing she could not figure out was how not to irreparably damage the lives of her kids and husband. She did not want to return to her husband, but did not know how to leave, either.

Samantha's husband did not make it easy for her. He pleaded, cajoled, and even threatened her with a life that would shrink to "the size of a postage stamp," with people shunning her if she should leave him. Whenever he was sad and reasonable, Samantha felt even more terrible. People who knew them as a couple always judged her as a bad wife and mother. But as Samantha knew within, with David, she had rediscovered who she was. Finally, it was her counselor who gave her the strength to break the news to her children, a move that did not happen without its consequences. Her son, who had left for college in Cairo, would not speak to her for a year afterward. Her daughters were speechless with shock and distanced themselves.

Finally, Samantha left for the US, leaving her husband's London home for good. At her hometown, the judgment was still harsher, with people picking sides, avoiding her, and averting their eyes when they met her. When she spoke to her therapist, he only said, "Don't let people punish you for choosing your happiness."

A little at a time, Samantha worked on herself and slowly understood that she would survive the ordeal. Believe it or not, Samantha and David made it. They continued to have a loving partnership based on equality, mutual love, and respect, 12 years after the incidents narrated here (Silva, 2023).

You may say that Samantha in the story turned out to be the "betrayer," a departure from the other stories in this book, where we only discuss women who have been abandoned, abused, or deceived. You may judge her for breaking up her family life and probably that of David's, and yet, there is also the niggling suspicion about whether her husband had ever truly fully allowed her to grow as a person. Though she refrains from criticizing him, she does make subtle references to his "dalliances." Even the manner in which he reasons with her to stay behind seems manipulative at best.

Whatever the truth of the affair may be, Samantha knew that staying back with her husband would constitute a greater deception than leaving him, and at least she deserves credit for having been honest about that.

The Importance of Therapy

Whether you are the betrayer or the betrayed, coming to terms with your new situation, will always take time, effort, and understanding. This is why therapy—whether you choose to go to a professional for help or work on yourself on your own—is essential for your healing. We shall look at some of the things that may seem confusing but necessary while undergoing this phase of life.

The Effort

Don't be fooled into thinking that the worst is behind you. The true aftermath of a betrayal generally hits you after it has happened, and when you are trying to make sense of it. A lot of physical energy and mental courage will have to go into understanding, processing, and accepting what has happened. At times, you will blame yourself, while at others, you will find your partner's behavior unacceptable. During the process, it is necessary to place the blame where it is due. Just as you may condemn the betrayal, you will also need to own the mistakes that you have made and genuinely make a reparation for them.

Facing the Consequences

However the situation may have played out, there are always consequences to accept. There may be family members, especially children, in the equation whose feelings will need to be considered. There are also the logistics that will need to be worked out—who will stay where, how will finances be handled, who will take charge of the children, and so on. Even if these work out somehow, there are your own emotions and feelings to settle.

If you find yourself betrayed, you

- may experience trauma. As experts suggest, the discovery of betrayal triggers your brain into a primal state of fear and doubt. It is natural for you to keep thinking in circles, trying to assess the situation and process the information. Our past is the only part of our lives that we can access and therefore, it is natural for us to keep revisiting it in the hope that something could have been done to prevent what happened. However, this fixation should be only a phase of trying to find a balance. If we get stuck in it, it could damage the very fiber of our existence.

- are entitled to ask for changes in the relationship dynamic. If your partner has violated the terms of your relationship, then it is perfectly justified for you to ask for changes. These measures should not be with the intention of punishing or humiliating your partner but to seek security and rebuild trust. For instance, you can ask that bank accounts should be made operable by both you and them, social media handles should be made more transparent, or phones should be unlocked. This will help you to feel safer and your partner will feel less tempted to prioritize anybody else over their family.

If you are the betrayer, then, you

- owe your partner the truth, whether or not you intend to save the relationship. Like with Samantha, if you have been the cause of what seems like a betrayal, you need to talk to your partner at the earliest, explaining the situation, your actions, and what you intend to do. You owe them an explanation, assuming they have been honest with you all along. You need to give them a chance to overcome their trauma and be able to trust you. If you plan to leave, then they deserve a heads-up about why it happened.

40

- can't expect an equal standing right away. Just as their betrayal would have shocked or hurt you, you need to be prepared for the consequences of your actions. Give them time to adjust to the new reality, and don't be quick to jump onto the wagon of defensiveness. No matter how justified you may feel, you must treat them with empathy and acknowledge the role you played in the breakdown of your relationship.

Not every relationship will survive a betrayal, so both you and your partner need to be prepared for that possibility.

You Decide Your Happiness

Healing comes when you decide to find happiness the way you want to. People around you will have many opinions about what happened. However, the only two people absolutely involved in the equation are you and your partner. You need to decide which way your happiness lies—whether together or separately. As Samantha's therapist told her, you don't need to allow others to punish you for choosing to be happy. You don't owe them anything. Yes, you do bear a responsibility to communicate your decisions to your spouse and children, but ultimately, your choice should be based on what you want rather than what you think is expected of you.

Take Responsibility for Your Actions

Wherever you think an apology is warranted to your partner, be sure to tender it. This does not in any way mean making yourself a doormat and taking on blame that wasn't yours to begin with. It only means being more honest with yourself.

In fact, go one step ahead and be the bigger person in offering your apology first, even if you feel your partner made the bigger mistake. You can communicate that though you are sorry for your part in the collapse of the relationship, you do not condone the hurt they have caused you or believe that you were the only one at fault. If you feel that an apology in return is not forthcoming, then that is your cue to leave with an unburdened conscience. Taking responsibility for your share of the problems is your burden, while how it is received is not your concern.

Time, Peace, Love, and Healing

As you navigate the pain of grief or betrayal, remember that with time, you'll gain perspective. You'll come to understand that happiness is powerful enough to transform everything, even if it feels like you have to lose everything to get there.

If and when love comes later again in life, it will bring an opportunity for growth, for building a life with intention, and for finding friendship and equality in partnership. You might find something that isn't always present in relationships born out of passion or societal expectations.

This kind of happiness won't be the exhausting work that many believe relationships mandatorily have to be, nor a rollercoaster of highs and lows. Instead, it will be a quiet, steady contentment, the kind that blossoms when two people are truly at peace with one another. And because of that, it will be a love that endures, a love that expands—big enough to envelop even children in the equation, who, with their own wisdom, will see the unhappiness of the past and recognize the peace in the present.

Some questions and quick pointers that you can ask/remind yourself as you begin and grow in your healing are:

- Do you believe you will always remain the sum of your actions in the past? What have you done with the knowledge you gained from your experiences?

- Are you rushing into new things—venture, relationships, or anything else? Have you first taken the time to understand yourself fully?

- Not everyone may agree with your choices. Keep people who respect (not necessarily agree with) your actions close, while removing toxic people from your life. Are you doing enough to stand up for yourself today?

- Do you trust yourself with your life? Are you at ease taking responsibility for all your life choices, including the not-so-great decisions you make?

Chapter 7:

Healing After Much Worse

Than Betrayal

I could never hurt him enough to make his betrayal stop hurting.
And it hurts, in every part of my body.
—Veronica Roth

Jenifer Faison often wondered if she was living a fairy tale romance. It had been seven years since she had reconnected with her high school sweetheart, and it was the ideal marriage. Her husband, Spencer Herron, was a teacher and was the epitome of a gentleman—kind, generous, charming, and the "perfect" husband. However, everything changed the day the police came into their Georgia home and arrested him. Jenifer couldn't believe the things they said about her husband. He had not only been a serial womanizer, but had also sexually assaulted female students at school! The web of lies and deceit he had woven around her life left Jenifer questioning whether she had ever truly known this man at all.

She had first met Herron at college and briefly dated him before parting ways with him. He had moved on, married, had kids, and it was only after his first divorce they reconnected via Facebook. Jenifer assumed what they had was a mature and loving relationship. She, who was a well-known TV producer by then, lost no time in accepting his proposal, moving in with him, and even opening a wine bar together.

After his arrest, just when she thought, there wasn't anything worse to come, she got access to his laptop where the things she saw horrified her. There were multiple nude photos of different women and even records of his chats and emails with them. He had used porn, escorts, and almost any form of sexual service available online to meet his needs. There was even evidence to suggest that he had cheated on her during their wedding week.

Meanwhile, Herron's student, Rachel, was being victim blamed and disbelieved. Nobody could visualize the two-time winner of the Teacher of the Year Award misbehaving with his students. Rachel went from a happy, excited, bubbly student to a sad, withdrawn, angry person who did not feel she deserved any good in her life.

Later, Jenifer would connect with Rachel on a podcast episode she hosted about her husband's criminality, thanking Rachel for her bravery in speaking out against the predator he was.

However, it took years of work for Jenifer to crawl out of the black hole, which had seemingly consumed her in the aftermath of her husband's huge betrayal. (Weintraub, 2023).

Dealing With Multiple Betrayals

Jenifer's story is not just about adultery. It reveals a much more sinister tale of sexual assault and grooming of young victims, whose only fault had been to repose their trust in the authoritative, and seemingly wonderful figure of their teacher. Spencer Herron was not the person he appeared to be—a fact that would torment his ex-wife for years to come. Worse than a single betrayal is multiple betrayals by a person you are committed to.

Sometimes, in the aftermath of deception, you can't really recognize your spouse or partner. *Who were they really? How did they do this to me? Why did they treat me differently? How did I not catch on to what was happening?*—These are just some of the questions that will negate any notion of mental peace.

In addition to this personal trauma you undergo, there could be people's conjecture that you may have colluded in abuse with your partner, when you were just oblivious to their double life—something that you yourself could be struggling to understand. Many people will doubt that you were as much a victim as your partner's other victims.

Research suggests that 20-23% of men and 13-19% of women resort to infidelity in committed relationships, with the rates being higher when it comes to self-reported emotional cheating (Street (Ed.), 2024). As such, a "double life" may not be as uncommon as you may imagine (Sherman, 1992). More commonly, most people have separate public and private selves—even normal well-adjusted people behave differently when they are alone, and when in company. However, this duality in personality can spin out of control when somebody can't reconcile the two halves of their personae. This is when a double life results in criminal behavior.

In an instance such as this, it is extremely important for you to absolve yourself of blame. No matter what society thinks, you know the truth. Your partner could have been such a seasoned liar and trickster that you fell prey to their tales. You knew nothing of their other life to have "enabled" them in their dark pursuits. In short, there is only one person to blame—them. They alone are responsible for their wickedness. You may also find peace in the knowledge that, most likely, you were not your partner's only victim. They could have ensnared and deceived many others like you over the years.

Some things that you may want to consider immediately after a betrayal of such a huge nature could include:

- **Therapy:** Agreed that you had no part to play in the terrible affair. However, you are now left with having to pick up the pieces and rebuild your life. This can be as hard as it is painful. Therapy will help you bring yourself back in focus. Instead of directing your energy at the person who created all the havoc, therapy will give you the time and space for you to center yourself in the scheme of things. A therapist will gently nudge you back into things that hold meaning for you.

- **Support system:** Lean on family members or friends to get you through the worst days. These are people who love you unconditionally and don't judge you for what happened. People who genuinely care for you will not let you down and will love you irrespective of where you are at the moment. They will ensure you eat and rest well through the days when caring for yourself seems impossible. Think of how you would have supported them had the crisis been theirs. Don't be ashamed to reach out when you need help.

Always remember that your story was real because you felt and experienced your side of the tale differently from the general narrative that has been woven around your life.

Your Story Was Real

At times, it is extremely hard to correlate the two lives your partner led and come to terms with what they did. You may blame yourself for not having realized their "real" nature. And yet, the fact is that what you experienced was just as "real" as their horrible deeds. You may feel hurt and embarrassed about the time and effort you took to be in this relationship. However, you behaved exactly as a sane person in love did, and there is no shame in that.

You couldn't have discovered them at their game because they had taken so much effort to keep their actions hidden from you. They played the part of the kind and genial spouse to the extent that it might have become second nature to them. You could not have seen the "red flags" because they behaved differently around you, and probably were a different person with you.

Probably, they themselves believed that their generosity to you made up for the evil in their soul. Whatever their motivations were, you are not required to make sense of them. You don't have to "figure out" why they did it. As far as you are concerned, you experienced their love in a harmonious environment because that's what they wanted you to believe. Your story and experience are real, no matter the ending. What matters now is not dwelling on what and why it happened, but taking charge of your life again.

You can use your experience to educate yourself and the people around you. Until your story happened, it may have seemed improbable or far-fetched in your life. You may never have thought that somebody could be such an expert deceiver. But now that you are wiser, you can take stock of your options and decide how you want your life to proceed.

Your story counts, not just because retelling it from your perspective may be therapeutic and cathartic, but also because it contains a cautionary tale for other women like you out there. Somebody somewhere might be saved with the insights from what happened to you. Turn your victimhood into victory for yourself and others abused like you.

Chapter 8:

Not All Betrayal Looks the Same

Everyone suffers at least one bad betrayal in their lifetime. It's what unites us.
The trick is not to let it destroy your trust in others when that happens.
Don't let them take that from you.
–Sherrilyn Kenyon

When Kathleen found out that her husband was a porn addict, it shattered her life. She did not want to accept that her perfect family and the lives of her two wonderful little kids were destroyed. While her immediate thought was that her husband and their family needed help, he was busy blaming her pregnancies for his loneliness and addiction. However, Kathleen realized later that her husband was addicted to porn even as a child. His condition certainly had very little to do with her.

Kathleen tried to stay strong as her husband dabbled in recovery and often went back to his ways. She did not want to break up her family and, besides, she did not realize that his behavior was abuse. Recovery and therapy were slow, with good and bad days. She held on for nearly 15 years before it finally dawned on her that her husband had done little to curb his tendencies. That's when they got separated—a move for which he continued to blame her.

Kathleen's turning point came when she stopped seeing her husband as "having a condition," and started seeing him as an emotional and psychological abuser who was playing with her feelings. Nobody told her that porn addiction in a marriage was also abuse. The focus of therapy and even that of the church members in whom she confided was always to "help" her husband. They often tried to justify his addiction in terms of his rough childhood. In the meantime, Kathleen felt like she was being blamed for his problem, when he was unwilling to work on himself.

Her husband went on to badmouth her to the entire community, painting Kathleen as a terrible wife and mother who failed to support him through his so-called illness. She could no longer go to her usual church and felt people looking down upon her. This abuse was now via third parties, as if the primary abuse via her husband was not enough. Kathleen felt that this secondary abuse was worse than what she had suffered at the hands of her husband.

Kathleen, with the help of a local abuse shelter, realized that she was being manipulated, abused, and shamed for something that she had very little control over. For the first time, instead of material related to porn addiction where she should "support" her spouse, she actively searched for resources to help herself get out of the abuse and trauma. She knew her anger was justified and that she had given him a lot of time to change. The problem wasn't with her or the nature of their marriage, but with him and his addiction. She remains convinced, and rightfully so, that his actions constituted infidelity and abuse. She still struggles with community members and former friends who believe that she has been too harsh on her husband (Kathleen, n.d.).

Your Definition of Betrayal May Differ

It is natural that others may not see a betrayal in the light you do. For instance, a partner addicted to pornography may not have had physical contact with a third person, and yet their emotional detachment stemming from their use of online sex can indeed constitute an act of trust violation. The fact that they are investing their sexual energies in a source different from their spouse or committed partner is in itself an act of infidelity.

Secondly, once porn addiction is identified as a problem in the marriage, the partner responsible for the breach of trust has to work on themselves and ensure there is progress in their behavior, attitude, and interaction with the other partner. Simply playing the victim card and blaming past or present people and situations does not absolve them of the responsibility they owe their relationship. Whenever they fail to keep their promises—more online transparency or increased interaction with the spouse—they continue to betray their relationship, partner, and family.

Thirdly, many people who resolve to work on themselves will seem like they are doing the work in the eyes of the people around them. They will go to therapy, take part in community service, say the things expected of them, and show what looks like genuine remorse, and yet, when push comes to shove, they may not have changed all that much in the things that count. They may still watch pornographic content, only hide their tracks better. They may still emotionally and sexually withdraw from their partners, giving excuses as to why they can't show up for the other person. They may continue to gaslight or manipulate the partner into thinking that they are at fault for the lack of progress in the other person's behavior.

Added to the suffering that you may experience in a relationship such as the above, you may find it incredibly hard to withstand the constant scrutiny of "well-wishers" wanting to know why you still seem unhappy with a partner, who seems to have changed outwardly. Again, more pressure is put on you to make you feel guilty or inadequate as the partner who is not supportive enough or creates unnecessary drama. All the while, you may be racking your brains to think what more you can do to help your partner, with whom you may have reached an impasse.

You Don't Need People's Validation

The moral of the story is this: If you feel you may be being abused, you probably are being abused in your relationship. Trust your gut in this matter, because outsiders cannot see everything happening in your relationship as you do. Your partner may also be lying and manipulating them as he does you. Therefore, they are not the best judges of what is truly happening inside your home.

A person may have had a very difficult childhood lacking love and affection. While this is sad, and you may sympathize with them, it does not justify their betrayal of your trust. They cannot use past or present situations or people as crutches to keep repeating the same mistakes over and over, expecting you to keep forgiving them forever.

Emotional and/or physical detachment from one's family is also a form of abuse. Parents and partners, when they sign up for these roles, have a responsibility to show up for their kids and significant others. Hardly anyone is forced into a family life. If your partner wants the privilege of continuing to be a part of your family unit, then they need to step up, be more transparent, do the work, and show that they are willing to change.

Apart from the objectification of human bodies and desires that pornography glorifies, it also sets up unrealistic expectations of sex from one's significant other. Its addictive and distractive nature makes people lose sight of the important things in life such as family ties, work, and meaningful rest and recreation. This is also why pornography addiction is more than just an addiction that destroys the person engaging in it. It is abuse on the partner and people who have to navigate its negative side.

When a person's destructive habits tie you down or impact your life negatively, you have no obligation to turn a blind eye to it or live a lie for the sake of their comfort. Religion, certain "moral codes," and even some forms of counseling may ask you repeatedly to put the other person before you. However, there is no saving anyone, without saving yourself first.

At times, you may need to relearn boundaries so that you can identify abuse for what it was. At such a crossroads, what you may need more than "counseling to set your family life right" could be trauma and abuse therapy for yourself. Be vigilant about your needs.

Self-preservation demands that you stand up for yourself and talk to the other person, making them listen to your concerns. If they ignore you or refuse to change their habits, then you have every right to walk out of the relationship. On the other hand, if they admit their mistakes and show the willingness and commitment to change, it is up to you to decide whether they deserve another chance.

Despite your best foot forward, if you find that there is no real change in the person or that they are lying and manipulating again, it becomes imperative for your own physical and mental well-being to leave.

Some questions that you may want to answer before you make up your mind regarding the next course of action could be:

1. How deeply addicted is your partner? Are they capable of rational thoughts, decisions, and choices?

2. Would it be more helpful for you to step back and let your partner face the consequences of their addiction, rather than cover up for them?

3. What would the above consequences be, and would they impact your well-being, too?

4. What part of the addiction do you want to control most? Do you think that this will be realistically possible?

After giving all the pros and cons enough deliberation, be confident in the decision you make, whether or not it meets societal expectations.

Chapter 9:

Nobody Need Tolerate Narcissism

Narcissus weeps to find that his Image does not return his love.
–Mason Cooley

Alex endured 30 years of abuse from her narcissistic husband. When they initially met, she thought of him as a "dream come true." However, certain behaviors of his unsettled her over time. She often brushed these off as his work stress. It took years for her to see that he was manipulating her into believing that he was her "soulmate" and that nobody else would want her. He flew into rages whenever she did something that displeased him. So she learned the art of walking on eggshells around him. She tiptoed and whispered, hiding her personality, just to avoid a conflict. She learned to make dinner just as he liked it and fulfilled all his requests immediately so as not to face the consequences. She thought of it all as her husband's "short fuse," and not as his manipulative nature. It was confusing and frightening, and she constantly doubted herself.

To neighbors and community members, he put up the facade of the ideal husband so that they never saw the real him. Whenever somebody came close to suspecting the truth, he would cut all ties with them. Alex never had a support network and felt isolated. He hid his financial troubles from her under the guise of "bank trouble" or a "problematic employer." He blamed everyone else, but never admitted his own excessive spending habits.

It was only after a friend introduced her to a podcast on abuse and betrayal that Alex realized what her husband had been up to all these years. She understood he had abused her dedication and sincerity. Finally, she found the strength to leave him.

Even years after leaving and feeling safe, small things remind her of the years of neglect she faced. She only wishes she had stood up for herself sooner and told him, "You're not treating me like this!" (Alex, 2024).

Why Leaving Can Seem Difficult

Alex's story is a classic case of being stuck with a narcissist. Her husband blamed her and criticized her to get her to toe the line. He would then apologize to her and make her believe his remorse was genuine, only for the entire cycle to repeat itself endlessly. Over time, his manipulation eroded her self-confidence and made her feel inadequate and insufficient to the extent that she doubted her capabilities.

Identifying a narcissist for who he is at the earliest is important. The earlier we recognize their symptoms and traits, the easier it becomes to extricate ourselves from such a relationship. The more we wait, the more difficult the whole process will become.

According to the criteria described by the American Psychiatric Association, a narcissist will exhibit some or most of the traits below:

- They feel entitled to special treatment and expect others to comply with their demands.

- They have an inflated sense of self-importance and expect recognition as superior, even without achievements to justify it.

- They constantly seek admiration and attention.

- They exaggerate their talents and accomplishments.

- They are fixated on fantasies of power, success, beauty, brilliance, or finding the perfect partner.

- They believe they are superior and only associate with people they perceive as equally special.

- They take advantage of others to achieve their own goals.

- They lack empathy and are unwilling or unable to acknowledge the needs and feelings of others.

- They act envious of others while also believing that others are envious of them.

- They display arrogant or conceited behavior.

Though it may seem obvious that living with such a person is problematic to both your physical and mental well-being, you would be surprised at the number of women who stick to their narcissistic partners. There are several reasons for this, such as (Firestone, 2022):

- **Fear:** Narcissists are experts in fearmongering. Some of them are physically, emotionally, or verbally abusive. Others are manipulative in making you believe that without them, you are incomplete or will never find anybody else who will truly value you as much as they do. Many victims, fearing angry reprisals or the prospect of being alone, choose to stay in the relationship.

- **Hope:** Being charismatic and charming, narcissists can make elaborate apologies and go to any lengths to make it seem like they understand their mistakes and are genuinely sorry for them. They offer just enough hope to make you believe that giving them another chance will repair the relationship. However, they don't intend to change. They will repeat their behavior and expect you to forgive them over and over.

- **Cognitive dissonance:** Cognitive dissonance is the negative thinking patterns that all of us pick up and exhibit from time to time. Narcissists are highly attuned to your particular type of dissonance and work on it, until you are convinced that you are not good, smart, beautiful, or talented enough. They keep you hooked on their validation, causing you to forget who you once were and gradually become a shadow of them. You will begin telling yourself that their control over you is only them being protective and loving of you.

- **Narcissistic trauma bonding:** Narcissists generally follow a pattern in attaching themselves to a person. This cycle includes (Greenberg, 2018):

➢ Stage 1: "Love bombing"—The narcissist overwhelms you with affection and constant validation to make you feel seen, heard, and loved.

➢ Stage 2: Building trust and dependency—You begin to believe their love is lasting, and you come to rely on them for emotional support and approval.

➢ Stage 3: Onset of criticism—They slowly withdraw their affection and validation, replacing it with criticism and blame. Their demands on you increase.

➢ Stage 4: "Gaslighting"—They convince you that the problems are your fault, insisting that if you only trusted them and followed their lead, they'd return to loving you. They manipulate your reality, making you question your perceptions.

➢ Stage 5: Establishing control—Confused about what to believe, you start to think the only way to restore the initial affection is by complying with their demands.

➢ Stage 6: Resignation and erosion of self—The situation deteriorates further. When you attempt to resist, the abuse intensifies. You become desperate for peace and for the conflict to end. You feel lost and unhappy, and your self-esteem is at its lowest point.

➤ Stage 7: Dependency—Your loved ones may express concern for you. You recognize how harmful the situation is, but you feel unable to leave because this person has become your entire world. Your focus is entirely on regaining their affection.

A narcissist plays by giving you love, affection, and respect intermittently and unpredictably. You no longer know how they will react to your actions, and model yourself always to win their appreciation and love. Over time, they will "groom" you to become what they want. The worst part of loving a narcissist is that they don't love anybody but themselves and will be the last person to admit that they have a problem.

Why Leaving Might Be Necessary

Unless it is with the aid of therapy, a narcissist is unlikely to change their behavior patterns. Due to their extraordinarily high sense of self-regard, a narcissist is unlikely to seek or stay committed to therapy. This means that without them being ready, willing, and committed to change, nothing—including your love—can ever change their nature for the better. Forget trying to "cure" them, and instead, focus on your health, safety, and happiness.

They may try to convince you that they'll change, leading you to believe their love is genuine, when in reality, this deception is just another part of their scheme to keep you hooked on the constant push and pull off their affection.

The repeated cycles of their waxing and waning attention will psychologically and physically harm you, causing you stress, anxiety, depression, and insomnia. In fact, in a toxic relationship, victims experience (Why Is Leaving a Narcissist so Hard?, 2022):

- fatigue and a lack of energy

- difficulty sleeping or oversleeping

- a noticeable change in appetite

- Persistent sadness or a low mood

- struggles with concentration and mental clarity (brain fog)

- guilt or worthlessness

- losing interest in activities once enjoyed

Clearly, it is in your best interest to walk away if the person you love doesn't care for your security and peace.

Stop trying to hold a narcissist accountable because they will perhaps never turn around their lives. There is a reason narcissism has been branded a personality disorder in psychiatry, and a strong possibility they will never change. It would be better for you to watch out for yourself. Similarly, you don't have to spend your time and energy wondering how and why they became who they are. It could be genetics or the way they were brought up. The fact is, you can't undo the damage that has happened to them—not without their consent and willing participation, at any rate. You can, however, prevent further damaging yourself mentally by stepping back from their turmoil. Focus on what you can control.

Leaving a narcissist is a tumultuous process of ups and downs where you keep doubting yourself and the wisdom of your choices. You may wonder if you are being fair to them and yourself by leaving them. There may be tranquil phases in the relationship where you feel more hopeful about lasting change, only to realize that nothing has changed or will change.

You may still find yourself loving parts of them and feeling sad about it. But remember that you can't help someone incapable of helping themselves. If you decide to leave, you don't need their "permission" or "blessing." This is something you have to do for yourself.

You may feel upset about the time you have wasted and wonder if you have anything left in yourself, or whether you can truly give yourself and others another chance. All these conflicting thoughts may keep you wanting to go back to your abuser.

Some things that you can do if you know that you are in a toxic relationship with a narcissist include:

- Find a support network of family and friends with whom you can openly share your experiences. Even if your significant other is gaslighting you, these people can offer a clearer perspective on what you're going through.

- Plan a safe exit strategy for yourself:

  o Identify a secure location to go before leaving your current situation.

  o Collect essential documents, such as your ID or driver's license, passport, birth certificate, educational certificates, marriage license, and financial records.

  o Plan how you will support yourself financially.

  o Ensure you have enough time to gather the necessary items before you leave.

  o Keep emergency hotline and authority contact numbers handy in case you find yourself in any kind of danger.

- Therapy is not just for the narcissist, it may be equally vital for you. Even after coming out of the relationship, you will need to heal the scars of your wounds before you can truly embrace your own identity again.

- Stop keeping track of their movements. Narcissists have the ability to move on quickly, no matter how hard they tried to convince you about their love for you. This will be doubly painful as you try to cope with your own hurt. Stop trying to contact them or being available for them when they reach out to you. You can go ahead and even block them on social media. The less you get sucked back into their game, the more you will find yourself.

- Engage professionals like lawyers, or friends, family members or others where a complete lack of contact with the narcissist is not possible. Where there are joint assets or children in the question, you may still have to "deal" with the person who so intimately destroyed a part of you. In such cases, be strong and calm and let others have discussions with them. You can also insist that you won't meet your abuser alone.

Finally, be kind to yourself. You have lost a lot of time being extremely hard on yourself, trying to cater to somebody else's vision. Now is the time to build your own voice and personality. Nobody can guarantee that it won't be painful, but beyond this temporary pain, lies a lifetime of peace and joy in knowing that you made the right move at the right time.

Chapter 10:

Finding Balance After

Financial Infidelity

I'm not upset that you lied to me, I'm upset that from now on I can't believe you.
—Friedrich Nietzsche

Valerie Rind talks of her experience with financial infidelity and betrayal from her husband matter-of-factly. She describes it as when one partner in a committed relationship hides their assets or liabilities from the other. In other words, a partner who hides their credit card debts or excessive shopping habits from the other person because of the fear of being dumped is guilty of being financially unfaithful.

Her husband kept the secret for a decade before she discovered it. When Valerie married Mark, an architect, he was living in a modest condo. Theirs was a love match, and Valerie, not being very materialistic, hadn't paid much attention to the details as long as their basic needs were met. When the condo began to feel cramped, they decided to rent a more spacious apartment until she completed law school and secured a job. Meanwhile, the condo was intended to provide a steady stream of rental income until they found their dream home. The plan was to eventually sell the condo to help finance their future home.

When Mark lost his job, Valerie suggested he should sell the condo to meet their expenses. She couldn't understand why he would resist this advice so vehemently. To her horror, she realized a little later that Mark had never owned the condo. He had been a renter when they met. Valerie realized they would never be able to buy a home with no assets to sell. Mark had deliberately misled her into believing in a future that was now impossible to conceive. Sadly, Valerie had made the decision to loan him money from her savings to finance his architectural consultancy, which went bankrupt around the time she decided to leave him.

She eventually moved out at a time he was off out of town and told him of her decision to leave him via a call. She wasn't sure if he would react angrily or use emotional appeals to make her stay. However, she knew she couldn't trust him again. She had already called a divorce lawyer and changed her will. When she called him and broke the news to him, she heard a long gasp. Mark knew that all was over.

For the next year, all Valerie had was a stable job at a law firm and her good sense to live within her means and take pleasure in the simple joys of life. With patience, courage, and hard work, she eventually managed to rebuild her life. She turned her life around and used this debacle to help others manage their personal finances (Rind, 2016).

Financial Infidelity Can Scar, Too

While money alone shouldn't be the sole measure of a person's values, the truth is that it plays an essential role in our lives. We rely on it to buy food, cover essentials, and secure a place to live—whether we rent or own. Just as with other aspects of a relationship, our views on money, assets, and liabilities should align with those of our partner.

In most marriages, finances become joint after a point of time. In such a case, it is extremely important for both partners to know how much each one earns and spends. All of the following are examples of financial infidelity:

- **Maintaining secret accounts:** Not every marriage or relationship necessarily banks on a joint account. However, maintaining secret accounts or credit cards shows that one partner is being secretive about their spending habits. Apart from ruining family finances, such secrecy might also point to more sinister intentions such as funding an addiction, illegal activity such as gambling, or an affair.

- **Hiding large purchases or transactions:** Once in a while all of us are guilty of buying something a little outside of our budget. But when this becomes a constant in a relationship, and when the person doing it keeps this hidden from their significant other, it points to a larger problem. It could mean compulsive spending or money spent for a purpose they know the other will not approve of. To keep up with this kind of expenditure, some people may even take loans, jeopardizing the entire family's fortune.

- **Spending joint savings:** Joint savings are generally put aside for some specific purpose such as buying a home, for kids' education, a future emergency, and so on. One person utilizing this resource for their own personal needs is a violation of the trust between the two partners.

- **Lying about income or expenditure:** This is one of the biggest red flags in a relationship. When a partner understates or suppresses expenses they incur or overstates their income, it is no longer a silly mistake they made and regret, but a deliberate attempt to conceal something they know is wrong and will upset the other person.

As with a secret addiction or having an affair, financial infidelity is a breach of faith. Whereas, as you looked to your partner for stability and security, they betrayed you. It could also affect the very foundation of your family and its future. As with any other form of infidelity, a financial one can leave you feeling hurt, angry, and frustrated. As with other types of betrayal, you may end up questioning who your partner really is when you discover they have compromised their financial credibility.

The Learning Curve

Whether you decide to stay in the relationship and make it work or to leave, financial infidelity has a lot to teach its victims. Never again must you take money for granted. We shall explore some ways to defend yourself against financial betrayal or to prevent it from happening again.

- Be wary of sudden changes in lifestyle: Always question how your partner is able to bring in new gadgets or afford things you could not earlier. A sudden downpour of gifts might also be a way to keep you complacent and an unknowing participant in the farce.

- Notice your partner's attitude toward money: Are they open and honest about assets and liabilities, or do they get defensive or evasive when talking about money? This is a vital clue in deciding whether they are trustworthy.

- Secrecy over devices: It is not only a partner who cheats physically, who might hide their screens and devices, it is also a person who may not want their partner to see the bank notices being sent to them.

- Discrepancies in financial statements: If you see large withdrawals or transfers from your or the joint account, immediately be on guard.

Not all financial cheaters start out wanting to trick the other person. Sometimes they do it thinking that they will surprise you with bigger and better returns, and panic when they have lost the initial capital. At other times, one or more of their insecurities pull them into a spending or gambling addiction. Whatever the cause might be, your job is not to deduce their intentions, but to protect your and your children's interests.

Assuming you have proof of your partner's financial infidelity, what next? In most countries, financial infidelity is also considered to be deceitful. The victim has every right to demand compensation or an adjusted settlement, depending upon the jurisdiction they come under.

Some steps you may want to keep in mind to move ahead are:

- **Gather information and evidence**

  - ○ **Review financial records**: Look through bank statements, credit card bills, and any other relevant financial documents to understand the extent of the financial infidelity.

  - ○ **Document irregularities**: Take note of any suspicious transactions or hidden accounts.

- **Seek professional guidance**

  - ○ **Financial advisor**: A professional can help you assess your financial situation and develop a plan to regain control over your finances.

  - ○ **Therapist**: A mental health professional can provide support as you process feelings of betrayal and decide how to move forward.

  - ○ **Legal advice**: If you're married or share financial obligations, consulting with a lawyer may be necessary to understand your rights and options.

- **Prepare for the conversation**

  - ○ **Approach calmly**: Plan a time to speak with your partner when you are calm and can discuss the issue without anger.

  - ○ **Be direct**: Present the evidence you've gathered and explain your concerns clearly.

○ **Set boundaries**: Communicate your expectations, such as full financial transparency, and set consequences if those boundaries are not respected.

- **In case you decide to stay: Promote "financial intimacy"**

  ○ **Decide together**: If your partner acknowledges their actions and is willing to work on rebuilding trust, you may consider financial counseling or therapy as a couple.

  ○ **Create a joint financial plan**: Set up shared access to accounts, establish a budget, and set financial goals together, slowly rebuilding trust.

  ○ **Track progress**: Regularly review your financial status together to ensure full disclosure.

- **Protect yourself financially**

  ○ **Open a separate bank account**: Ensure you have access to your own funds and financial resources.

  ○ **Change account passwords and access**: If necessary, secure your financial information to prevent any further losses.

  ○ **Build an emergency fund**: Start saving independently so you have a safety net if you need to leave the relationship.

- **Decide whether to stay or leave**

  ○ **Reflect on the relationship**: Consider if the relationship is worth saving and whether your partner shows genuine remorse and willingness to change.

- Prioritize your well-being: If trust cannot be restored, or if your partner continues to hide financial information, you may need to separate and prioritize your own financial security and emotional health.

- **Take steps to move on**

  - **Reach out to a support system**: Contact friends, family, or support groups who can provide emotional and practical help.

  - **Focus on self-care**: Practice self-care and engage in activities that build your confidence and independence.

  - **Plan for the future**: Set new financial and personal goals for yourself to help rebuild your life independently.

In accountancy, we often speak of the reconciliation of assets and liabilities. However, in the case of financial infidelity, you decide whether or not to reconcile yourself to the person who was responsible for it. Whatever you decide, be financially proficient so that you are never again at the mercy of anyone.

Chapter 11:

Embracing the Sisterhood

*Sisters in battle, I am shield and blade to you. As I breathe, your enemies will
know no sanctuary. While I live, your cause is mine.*
–Leigh Bardugo

Eryn's and Kristin's stories are intertwined in a sadly unalterable way.
Eryn's cheating husband was Kristin's cheating fiancé. Both the women
were duped by the same man and perhaps that is why they formed a
strong bond with each other. In fact, they realized that they weren't
even the only two women in his life!

Eryn tracked down the "other woman" as she thought of her at the
time. Initially, Kristin was "the enemy," the woman who had "torn
apart" Eryn's house, and she felt justified in wanting to punch or
humiliate her. Eryn always wondered what kind of selfish woman
would break apart a family to get the man she wanted. And yet, when
they met, she realized that the woman was conned just like she was by
the same man.

Eryn's husband had forged fake divorce papers to prove that his
divorce from her was almost finalized when he met Kristin. He had
also lied about multiple things to Kristin. He told her that his son had
an autoimmune disease, his wife (that is, Eryn) was bipolar, and that his
best friend had died in his arms during combat. The facts were that
their only son was strong and healthy, and Eryn had no medical history
of mental illness. Her husband had never been in active combat and his
best friend was alive and well! Apart from all the lies, the man used
Kristin emotionally and even asked for her help in his work as a
marketer. Finally, when the lies became too big, he broke up with
Kristin, devastating her. The man was as charming as he was inventive,
as the two women would discover.

In addition to all his follies, Eryn's husband from whom she was divorced by this time never apologized to Kristin. He never told her the truth and instead waited for her to find out everything on her own. Eryn suddenly felt, not angry, but a deep sadness for both of them—all because of one man's twisted lies, they had to suffer so much of unnecessary pain.

As Eryn thought about her ex-husband, she was filled with mixed emotions. On the one hand, she still shared kids with him and had very little savings to rely on because he had wiped their accounts clean. On the other hand, she could now pursue her life and career more authentically and preserve her self-confidence from his toxicity. Eryn hoped that her unexpected sisterhood with Kristin would bring them both the peace and closure they sought—and she was right! (Mile High Mamas, 2017).

Place the Blame Where Due

We often label the woman a man cheats with as the "homewrecker," the "other woman," or the "epitome of evil and selfishness." However, many times she is just as much a victim and a pawn in the game as the wife or committed partner is. If a man cheats on his committed partner, there is nothing holding him back from cheating on his "mistress" either.

Betrayers make a habit of painting a larger-than-life picture of themselves to confuse, lie, and manipulate their way into the lives of their victims. They either use tall tales of their prowess to impress their victims or worm their way in through sob stories meant to evoke sympathy. They suppress or minimize truths to entrap their victims. Just as their committed partner is deceived, several others might fall for their sugary words, only realizing the truth much later. A man who lies to his family will have no compunction about lying to the other people in his life. However, sometimes the lies will seem so genuine that they are hard to spot.

The golden rule to follow as a woman is not to encroach on a sister's turf. Never willingly submit to a man who you know is cheating on their partner, no matter how enticing their offer may seem. Do not enable cheaters, for they will do to you exactly what they have done to their partner or spouse. If you encounter such a man, keep your distance. And if he deceives you, step away from his lies and manipulation the moment you see through his tricks.

If you are the partner of such a man, refrain from blaming the "other woman" because the man who committed himself to you—body, mind, and soul—made a conscious choice to cheat on you. Nobody held him at gunpoint, forcing him into infidelity. Place the blame where it is due. There is only one person who betrayed you—him.

The Power of Sisterhood

There are several forms of intimacy. Most people box in intimacy as a romantic relationship, and yet, that is only a very narrow definition. The intimacy you share with a significant other is only one tiny part of the spectrum. Important as love may be for anyone, you must understand that the end of a romantic relationship need not necessarily mean the end of love for you. Intimacy means feeling close to someone, loved, appreciated, and respected as who you are. It means the other person "gets" you, even if they don't always agree with you. Such bonds don't have to be limited to blood, family, or romantic ties.

A random Google search for the word "sisterhood" will give you multiple results on women who have found incredible strength and resilience in their girl gangs. With other women we can share, cry, laugh, celebrate, and create. We're talking about women who will stand by you through thick and thin—even in the darkest times, when the whole world seems against you. These women will give you their physical, emotional, and moral support because most have been through rough patches just like the one you are facing now. What's even better, they will bring their valuable perspective and experience to your challenges, and through their stories you stand to gain a lifetime of wisdom.

Women are very emotionally intuitive, which makes it easier for them to understand another's pain, even if they haven't been through the exact situation. You only need to look at the number of TV soap operas that depict female friendships to understand how instrumental they are in shaping one another and how motivational such support can be.

Perhaps because women are often encouraged to be nurturers from an early age, you may find that many are less competitive or judgmental than men. This isn't to suggest that women shouldn't be go-getters—it's simply an observation of what is, rather than what ought to be. When you find a sister on your wavelength, you can talk to her without fearing judgment and censure. Sisters will also take pride in your achievements as if they were their own. Research suggests that while men bond with each other via shared activities like hitting the gym or playing a sport, women bond primarily through conversations (Carter, 2023). It is also very normal for women to discuss things that may be considered "gross" or "inappropriate" for men to discuss among themselves, like the last time they menstruated or aspects of physical intimacy with their partner. In short, relationships between women are very different from those between men, and those between men and women. Another study shows how the survival period of women with mortal diseases could be prolonged with supportive group therapy than if they were isolated (DeAngelis, 2002).

Therefore, even if you are only contemplating the health of your romantic relationship, actively seek out and widen your support network of sisters who can be there for you. What can you do about this? Let us try to look at some strategies to connect more with other women, whether it is to form personal or professional bonds:

- **Reflect on what you want from a sisterhood.**

  - Firstly, clarify your intentions—do you seek emotional support, professional connections, shared interests, or friendship?

  - Think about the values you want in these connections: authenticity, trust, growth, encouragement, etc.

○ Once you are clear about your stand on the above questions, you can start your work.

- **Join women-centered groups and communities**.

  ○ **Local and online groups**: Look for women's groups focused on interests like self-development, entrepreneurship, fitness, spirituality, or book clubs. Platforms like Meetup, Facebook Groups, or Eventbrite can help you find such communities.

  ○ **Non-profit organizations**: Volunteering or participating in causes related to women's rights, empowerment, or community development can introduce you to like-minded women.

  ○ **Hobby-based classes**: Enroll in classes such as yoga, art, dance, or cooking, where you can meet other women in a relaxed, supportive environment.

- **Foster genuine connections through vulnerability**.

  ○ Be open about your experiences and challenges (within your comfort level) to create space for authentic conversations.

  ○ Show genuine interest in others 'stories, offering empathy and support to build reciprocal relationships.

  ○ Avoid oversharing too quickly, but share enough so others feel comfortable opening up as well.

- **Engage in online sisterhood communities**.

  ○ Social media platforms like Instagram, Facebook, Reddit, and Twitter have women-focused communities and hashtags (e.g., #womenempoweringwomen, #sisterhood) which you can become a part of.

- Follow and interact with communities, share your journey, and support others' stories to establish connections.

- Participate in online workshops, webinars, or women's summits where you can engage with a larger network.

- **Create your circle.**

  - If you don't find a community that fits, consider starting your own group. It could be as simple as hosting a small gathering, organizing a book club, or creating a WhatsApp group for women with shared interests.

  - Invite women you meet through other activities and friends to join, and encourage everyone to bring someone along.

- **Seek out mentorship and offer support.**

  - Look for women who inspire you and reach out to them for advice, collaboration, or guidance.

  - At the same time, you can be a source of support for others. Sisterhood thrives when women empower each other.

- **Attend women's events, conferences, and workshops.**

  - Women's empowerment seminars, leadership conferences, or self-care retreats are great ways to meet and connect with other women who prioritize sisterhood.

- Approach these events with the intention to learn, connect, and support rather than just network.

- **Set boundaries and prioritize healthy connections.**

  - Be mindful of the energy you're bringing and receiving in relationships. Seek connections that feel uplifting and supportive, rather than draining or judgmental.

  - Recognize when a connection isn't healthy and step back if necessary, prioritizing your emotional well-being.

- **Practice consistency and patience.**

  - Building a network takes time. Consistently show up for events, follow up with the women you meet, and engage in conversations to deepen bonds.

Some final words of advice would be to exercise patience and allow connections to develop naturally; not every interaction will lead to a deep friendship, but over time, you'll find your circle.

Chapter 12:

Starting From Scratch

...if you want anything said, ask a man. If you want anything done, ask a woman.
—Margaret Thatcher

Natalie, a well-known YouTube influencer, tells us that she never really thought she would be starting over her life in her 50s. A younger Natalie would have assumed that by this time she would be financially independent with a thriving career and happily married with children. In fact, she is honest enough to admit to her viewers she wasn't even sure whether to record this particular video showcasing all her vulnerabilities as it did. She tells us that it was only her wish to support and strengthen other women like her that motivated her to be candid about things. She goes on to talk of the previous year when she coped with two devastating losses—the first loss was of her father and the second of her partner of 14 years, who had been in an affair with another woman for years before Natalie discovered it. She also found out via social media that her partner had started a business with his lover. When Natalie confronted him, he refused to talk to her and moved out. Natalie tells us how rejected and abandoned she felt in the aftermath of him leaving without an apology, truthful explanation, or closure. She also felt terrible that while she had been suffering through various health problems linked to her menopause, her partner had been seeing his lover behind her back. She had always thought of him as the love of her life, the man she would spend the rest of her life with.

Natalie affirms that her faster-than-anticipated recovery and her ability to smile through it all on most days is owing to her deep connection with God and the therapy she is undergoing. She talks about how therapy helped her see herself better. Her father's abuse of her mother and her being sent to a care home whilst her mother pulled her life together had all shaped Natalie's worldview and ideas on love. She had always been cautious about opening up to others, yet ironically, her worst fears still came true.

She also admits that it has not been all smooth sailing because there are days when the sadness catches up, and she asks herself questions like: Where did it all go wrong? How is it that she is 52 and leading such a life—what a mess?! She often feels that she lacks direction and purpose.

In spite of it all, Natalie has been doing her work. She shows up for her therapy, has been actively opening up to friends and family members whom she cares for, and taking joy in all the things she loves doing. She's even working on a project focused on housing for women—something deeply close to her heart. She's convinced that even greater things await her and that everything that's happened was part of a larger plan to shape her true self (*Starting life over at 52*, 2024).

Starting Over

Gratitude and patience are true lifesavers, whether or not you're in a relationship. They don't always come naturally; as humans, our first instinct is often survival, which can lead us to take things for granted over time. Cultivating mindful gratitude helps us appreciate what remains, even in the face of loss. For instance, you might have a home, a family, children, or a steady job that provides security. Maybe you're blessed with wonderful friends who support you. No matter how challenging life feels, there are positives—if you take the time to recognize them. Make it a habit to jot down these positives and consciously use them to nurture optimism. You might be surprised, but happiness often attracts luck, joy, and fulfillment.

Shift your mindset, slowly but steadily, from negativity to positive energy. This is easier said than done. When betrayed and let down, it is hard to get over the bitterness and anger of what your life could have been if that particular episode had not happened. It is also absolutely fine to mourn for all the "could have beens" in your life too—that is a part of the healing process. However, when these projected possibilities start weighing you down, you know it is time to let them go. As with happiness, you have to consciously reframe both your thoughts and language (because they shape one another) to ensure you give genuine people and opportunities a fair chance to be let into your life. If you hold your heart and mind closed, you will risk living a life mired in the past and floundering in possibilities that will never attain fruition.

Salvage whatever you can from the experiences you've had—whether it's your physical and mental health, your joy, or even your life itself. As cliché as it may sound, tough times are bends in the road, not dead ends. Take what lessons you can from each experience and strive to become better than before. Eat well, rest, and exercise so that your body can be a temple to beautiful thoughts and actions. Engage with ideas that may have been alien to you—not to change yourself altogether, but to broaden your mental horizon. New ideas and concepts may either spark recognition in you, or they may lead you to think up novel ways to perceive yourself and your situation. Therefore, read, talk, and observe more.

Find purpose. Chase a purpose and not another person. Human life has always been one of trying to find meaning and balance. No person without a purpose or a cause that fulfills them can ever be truly happy. This is why we have many turning away from jobs that merely pay well. Your motto should be to find things that allow you to feel engaged and useful. If some of these activities or pursuits can bring material wealth as well, then that is an added blessing. If you can find a job that feeds your hunger and simultaneously a hobby to feed your soul, then that will do too. Do whatever makes your soul sing, and ensure you don't have time to engage with regret and guilt.

(Re)Finding Hope and Reframing Negativity

Don't chase, but remain open to all that is to come: Remember how as a child you used to close your fists tightly on water or sand, only to find it flowing away? Hope and love are pretty much like that. You can have them around the things you do daily and retain optimism with an open heart. But chase them too hard, and they may just give you the slip. Hope and love are still in the cards for you—this is something you should believe in. It can and will happen when the time is right. This doesn't mean that you remain passive and shut off from all that life has to offer you, it simply means you do not to jump at every opportunity that arises. It means you weigh the pros and cons of what is on offer and take up only those that are worth your time, energy, and effort.

You are complete: Don't rely on another to "feel complete." You should be complete on your own, with or without a partner beside you. You are complete in your thoughts, deeds, and beliefs. If you find a loving partner in the future, that is wonderful, but you don't need them to define who you are or what you stand for. We are taught that pairing off is the natural way of life. Yet, to stand on your own and find your strength, resilience, and power is the real mark of coming into your own. Once this happens, nothing and nobody can take away your essence from you.

Your timeline is your own: Ditch the predefined "breakup timeline." There is no such thing. You can set your own pace and find peace earlier or later than you were hoping for, without feeling guilty. Even well-meaning friends and family members may push you to meet new people or to move ahead. However, you decide when and how to regain your inner peace. This doesn't mean that you do nothing, of course. You will still work toward happiness and engagements that bring meaning and joy in your life, but take it easy when you feel the need to. There is no pressure to be in the next relationship or to make a "dramatic" shift in your life, unless you are certain that you are prepared for them. You may also be tempted to make changes to your hairstyle and wardrobe, some of which could be truly empowering and some of which you may regret a little later. Therefore, stay away from drastic changes initially, and slowly consider your choices wisely. Instead of making hasty decisions, wait until you are peaceful and calm to decide which of your options you want to go ahead with.

Reframing negativity: Recurring negative thoughts are a challenge even in ordinary times. When pushed against a wall, the greatest pressure, at times, comes from within yourself. In Natalie's case above, she felt low, thinking that her life hadn't panned out as she would have expected it. This comparison between an idealized future and what is right now can spawn only frustration and despair. Instead, take your negative thoughts, one at a time, and rationalize them by gathering proof of them. You will be amazed at the lack of evidence for the negative thoughts you will come up with, forcing you to ditch them, and reframe them in a healthier and more honest manner.

Here are some examples to consider and reframe your own particular negative thoughts:

Negative thought	Questioning the "proof"	Reframed and positive thought
I have been nothing but a fool.	I loved a person who cheated on me. Does that make me a fool?	I am strong enough to have loved and let go when the time was right. I can only be stronger for the experience.
Nobody will ever love me.	I went through one breakup. Does that make me unlovable?	There are many who find me attractive, funny, and kind. I will eventually bond with the right person.
I have wasted my life.	I spent my energy and time on a venture/person that did not eventually work out. In what way does that make me a failure?	I will continue to keep my heart open to opportunities in the light of my experience thus far. I have learned, and my life is richer for it.

Negative thought	Questioning the "proof"	Reframed and positive thought
What will I do?	I have already done so much. (List all your achievements here.) Why won't I survive?	I will do whatever it takes to keep myself positive, light, and hopeful. I will neither be giddy in my expectations nor down in the dumps with despair.
What will people think/say about me?	What do I actually know about what people are thinking about me? Why should that bother me?	Genuine people will understand my situation and actions. Others are not worth losing sleep over.

Living through a breakup, especially one that involves a breach of trust, is an achievement in itself. Don't undermine yourself or your abilities based on hearsay and your assessment of yourself through other people's eyes.

Chapter 13:

Did I Make the Right Choice?

There comes a time in your life when you have to choose to turn the page,
write another book, or simply close it.
–Shannon L. Alder

Katie Bogen's story is one more about heartbreak than betrayal. She had reconnected with her childhood sweetheart, Tom, less than a year before they decided to tie the knot. A whirlwind romance had swept Katie right into the vortex of things. They began preparing wedding guest lists and making other arrangements when things started to unravel. One argument led to the next, and before she knew what was happening, she was calling him and telling him that she wasn't getting what she needed from their relationship. It was extremely hard for her to withstand the push-pull of the feelings she still had for Tom. She spent days ecstatic about having made the right choice, feeling sure he would crawl back to her, and then feeling hurt, numb, and afraid of having split up with him the rest of the time. It was unnerving that she, an avowed feminist, had let a small breakup get to her to such an extent. She couldn't understand why she felt so miserable.

When she couldn't take it anymore, she set out to find some scientific truths behind her feelings. She found that love, at times, mimicked addiction to drugs and that a sudden breakup could trigger withdrawal symptoms an addict might face when they stop using. She also found and rated a series of things that helped her get over her ex including cutting off all her hair, living a more health-conscious lifestyle, focusing on her career, catching up with friends and social engagements, blocking her ex on all social media, and getting back into the dating arena. She found that the most effective strategies that worked for her were reconnecting with old friends, putting her heart and soul into her work, and being part of social events again (Bogen, 2017).

Self-Discovery

After you lose someone whom you assumed would be a constant in your life, it is tempting to fall back into coping strategies that may do you more harm than good in the long run. For instance, you may take up drinking more regularly to take the edge off your sadness, or mindlessly hook up with people just to feel temporarily less alone. However, these defense mechanisms will not help you find yourself again. They will just numb your mind and body for a while.

Though people may ask you to "tough it out" and not feel it, it is quite impossible to make heartache less painful by simply suppressing or ignoring it. In fact, sadness of any kind has to be processed before one can make heads or tails of it. In other words, you need to feel your heartache and go through a grieving phase before you can feel stronger and more in control of yourself. Emotional acceptance of what you feel is not just okay, but a necessary part of the whole process.

However, try not to give in to the urge of simply curling up at home, binge-watching shows, and eating comfort foods. Yes, this is a good strategy on some days you feel you simply can't do anything else, but it cannot be the only way. Instead, you need to rely on a concrete action plan to make new memories. This will not take away the pain but will definitely push it aside. Experts say that the pain and grief of loss will never entirely fade, but it can be made more bearable with the richness of new experiences to surround the gaping hole. You can also try to consciously stay clear of previous memories by visiting new places and making new friends, unconnected to your ex.

The push and pull of feelings for someone you thought would be a part of your life forever is normal. When you are newly alone and vulnerable, you may idealize or romanticize the time you spent with them. But you can't keep succumbing to these feelings and thoughts forever, and delay your moving on. Therefore, every time you reach out for the phone intending to call or message them or answer their call, hit pause. Mindfully, go back to every single reason why you broke up with them. You can list out the detailed causes that led to the breakdown of your relationship. Going over this list should not be with the intention of beating yourself up, but so that you don't forget how unhappy you were being with that person. Cutting contact with your ex is, most times, quite effective to break the lingering spell they may hold over you. Though an "amicable separation" and "staying friends" may seem for the best, it could prolong the heartache unnecessarily, too. A clean break, including removing physical reminders such as old photos, messages, or letters from them, will give you the time to refocus your attention where it is truly deserved. A social media purge that will reduce your urge to keep stalking them online may also be desirable at this stage.

Though you may think yourself above it, never discount therapy without first giving it a try. It will help you rediscover your hobbies, passions, and talents and aid in framing your thoughts and feelings in more constructive patterns. The key is to find a person with whom you can build a comfortable rapport. They are an unbiased outsider who will neither sugarcoat things nor blame you for what happened, and might be relied upon to bring ideas that people closer to you and even you yourself may have missed. If you feel therapy makes you feel worse than you already did, you can always stop or seek a counselor more suitable for you.

We have touched upon self-care and getting involved in things that bring you joy. These could be anything from reading, writing, watching movies, date nights with yourself, tasting new food, gardening, traveling, or setting a new exercise or fitness routine. Though there is no need to go on the warpath and take on so much that your mind and body feel overwhelmed, there is also some wisdom in nudging yourself out of your comfort zone. Nobody who hasn't pushed themselves knows the limits of who they are and the potential they can reach. Thus, don't quit the things you start. Instead, keep at them with reasonable breaks and rest so as not to exhaust yourself too much. Approach everything new slowly and steadily, not burning yourself out trying to do it all at once.

Learning to Live Again

This survival mode you are in won't last forever. Let us look at some ways in which you can teach yourself the art of living once again.

Be More Social—Even If It Feels Forced

After a breakup, you might feel the urge to withdraw and isolate yourself, but this can often lead to a cycle of loneliness and sadness. Being social, even when you don't feel like it, is a powerful tool for healing.

Pushing yourself to attend social events, whether it's a friend's birthday party, a work gathering, or a casual get-together, is important. At first, it might not be enjoyable, and you might feel out of place. It's common to have moments where you compare yourself to others who appear happy and content. But with each event you attend, you give yourself the opportunity to rebuild social connections, rediscover hobbies, and create new experiences. Over time, the discomfort will lessen, and you'll find yourself genuinely enjoying the company of others again. Being around people, even if they're not your closest friends, can help you feel less alone and remind you that life continues to be full of possibilities.

Prioritize Your Health—Conscious Choices for Mind and Body

Breakups take a toll on physical health. It's easy to slip into unhealthy habits, such as overeating, not eating enough, or using food as a comfort mechanism. Exercise routines may fall apart, and sleep patterns may become erratic. However, making a conscious effort to prioritize your health is crucial for recovery and well-being.

Start with small steps—eat balanced meals that nourish your body, like fresh fruits, vegetables, and lean proteins. Avoid excess sugar or processed foods that can contribute to mood swings. Regular exercise, even if it's just a daily walk, can release endorphins that naturally elevate your mood and boost energy levels. When you exercise, you engage in a form of self-care that proves to yourself that you matter, reinforcing positive thoughts and reducing stress.

Sleep is another pillar of well-being that shouldn't be neglected. Aim for 7–9 hours of quality sleep each night. A restful night's sleep can significantly affect your mood and energy, allowing you to approach the day with a clearer mind and more resilience. If sleep has been a struggle, consider establishing a nighttime routine—limit screen time before bed, create a calming environment, and maybe incorporate practices like meditation, reading, or listening to calming music to help settle your thoughts.

Reconnect With Old Friends—Finding Comfort in Familiarity

Heartbreaks often leave you questioning your support system, and it's common to feel lonely even when surrounded by others. One way to counter this feeling is by reconnecting with old friends. These are the people who know you beyond the context of the relationship that just ended. They can remind you of your strengths, your quirks, and the life you had before the breakup.

Reaching out to old friends may feel awkward, especially if you haven't been in touch for a while, but it's worth the effort. Many times, these friends will be understanding and supportive, eager to reconnect and be there for you during this difficult period. Even if it's just a coffee meetup or a simple phone call, reconnecting can be therapeutic. These interactions offer a sense of safety and familiarity, providing comfort as you rebuild your confidence and sense of self.

It's also an opportunity to be honest and open about your feelings. Often, sharing your emotions with someone who understands you well can be incredibly healing. It validates your experience and reminds you that you're not alone in this.

Give Love a Chance Again—Slowly and on Your Own Terms

After a painful breakup, the idea of jumping into another relationship may feel daunting or even impossible. It's important not to rush into a new commitment until you're truly ready, but that doesn't mean you should shut yourself off from meeting new people. Exploring connections casually can help you heal by reminding you that love, affection, and companionship still exist in the world.

Taking small steps—like going on casual dates or simply interacting with new people—can help you rebuild your confidence and rediscover your interests outside your previous relationship. There's no pressure to find a perfect match or to rush into anything serious. Instead, focus on enjoying the process of getting to know someone new, learning from each interaction, and figuring out what you really want moving forward. The experience can be liberating and might reaffirm that while the past relationship was meaningful, it needn't define your future opportunities for happiness.

Healing takes time, and it's okay to move at your own pace. What's important is that you continue to make conscious choices that prioritize your well-being, allowing you to find happiness and strength in the life that lies ahead.

Chapter 14:

The Two Fs—Faith and

Forgiveness

Many people have trouble with forgiveness because they have been taught
that it is a singular act to be completed in one sitting. That is not so.
Forgiveness has many layers, many seasons.
–Clarissa Pinkola Estes

Venus Morris Griffin opens her interview by talking about her seven
amazing children, all between the ages of six and 26, and how they are
her greatest accomplishment, even though she feels she can't take
credit for them. She first shared her story on Humans of New York
about the ordeal she faced with her husband's conviction for child
molestation. But her story began much earlier than even that. It started
with her being raised by a mother who was a drug and alcohol addict.
Her mother used to shoplift, steal, and even file false insurance claims
to fund her addiction. As a small child, Venus remembers telling her
friends about her life and being told that her home stories sounded so
"wild." That's when she realized that not everyone had a similar
lifestyle and that her friends would soon think her a terrible liar if she
told them what was happening at home. Her dysfunctional family
included a brother who would go on to be fired from all his jobs and
jailed several times for stealing, and a sister who would later be
admitted to a mental asylum.

Venus knew enough of what she did not want from a family life. She
was always in a relationship, hoping her marriage and family life would
be different from the one she was raised in. When she met Tripp at
college, Venus was convinced he was the man of her dreams. He was
smart, the president of his fraternity, rich, goofy, and extraordinarily
handsome. With her traumatic background, she also probably lacked

the acumen to perceive what Tripp truly was. This was why she put up with his erratic and rage-fueled tantrums in their 20-year marriage, thinking that it was normal for a man to behave this way in a marriage. She also believed that his anger stemmed from the stress of having to take over his family business.

The turning point came for Venus when a woman with whom Tripp was having an affair called her and told her how abusive he had been. She also hinted that Tripp was spending all his money on prostitutes for years. To Venus's horror, she realized their bank accounts were empty and all their credit cards maxed out. When confronted, Tripp admitted to his sex addiction and checked himself into a rehab. But the worst revelation was to come when one of her own daughters told her that daddy had been behaving inappropriately with her. Venus felt ashamed that she had failed her own children. She left with her children and eventually divorced her husband.

Today, her husband is serving a 45-year sentence on child molestation charges. Venus is a successful realtor who cleared all her ex-husband's debts, and continues to be a great mother to her children, whom she considers her life and soul. She still writes to her ex-husband in prison and shares photos of her kids with him because she knows it is the human thing to forgive a man who is mentally ill. She feels it is her Christian duty to him, despite the awful things he has done to her and her family. After years of caring for her mother, she recently had her relocated to a separate apartment, where she continues to support her (Griffin, 2023).

Forgiveness

There is an old maxim that asks us to "forgive and forget." However, this is an insufferable and impossible ideal, especially where abuse and trauma are concerned. Even if one can work on themselves to forgive the person who has wronged them, forgetting is out of the question and even undesirable. Forgetting is akin to repressing memories and emotions till we don't feel them—something that goes against the very grain of therapy and healing. As we have maintained many times during the course of this book, healing involves experiencing and talking about the pain until we emerge stronger from it. It is like tempering or passing metals through fire when they emerge tougher.

But what about forgiving? Is it possible, and why would that be necessary? When a person commits a grave injustice unto you, being told to forgive them may sound a little unrealistic and even unsympathetic. Forgiveness could be the last thing on your mind. You may struggle with thoughts of revenge and torturing the person responsible for your pain. You may want them to suffer until they feel like you did. That's just the thing, though. You *assume* they are a rational person like you with feelings, emotions, and thoughts. What if they are incapable of feeling? What if they are far gone beyond feelings of humanity, justice, kindness, and even pain? What if their hell has already started even as they committed those terrible things against you? Why would you waste your remaining time and energy trying to wreak havoc on a person who is beyond redemption anyway?

There are many academic takes on forgiveness. While many therapists claim that forgiving yourself and your tormentor is necessary for healing, some say that self-forgiveness is mandatory while forgiving the other person is a subjective concern, varying from one victim to the next and their specific situation. (Balan, 2024). There is perhaps a way to reconcile both parts of the above argument.

Thoughts of revenge, resentment, and bitterness are a two-way street. They may keep you alive for the moment, thinking about your issue, but may also seem like an incredible burden to carry over time. A quote that has evolved over time rightly says, "Resentment is like swallowing poison and expecting the other person to die" (Quoteresearch, 2017). Constant hatred and anger will never allow us to grow in the direction we want to. Instead, it will keep us trapped in the past.

So, is forgiveness the only way to healing? Yes and no. Yes, we need to forgive ourselves and the part we (unwittingly, maybe) played in our own misery. We can't forever carry the guilt and shame of not having known or left sooner. The earlier we accept the mistake we made, come to terms with it, and resolve to be wiser and smarter in the future, the sooner we will heal ourselves. As for forgiving the abuser, that is something that is totally your own prerogative—even if religion or therapy tells you otherwise. You don't necessarily have to forgive the person for what they did, and you certainly must not forget what happened. However, ensure your decision does not keep you tied up in their misdeeds for a minute longer than is necessary because you may have already lost a lot of time giving them chances when they did not deserve it. Forgiveness, as we have already seen, is for you to release yourself from agony, and not for them. You may choose to forgive the person and not his sin, or you may forgive him entirely and decide to move on—this choice neither needs to be binary nor even made in a single timeframe. In every season of healing, you may feel differently about the person who hurt you and what happened to you—that is perfectly okay. As long as you are not stuck in the past but mindfully enjoying the present and looking optimistically at the future, you are good to go.

"Time heals all," a wise proverb reminds us. This doesn't mean that the pain will vanish or that you will or must forget the fire you walked through. It simply means that as your heart and brain expand to make space for newer, happier, and better memories, the old ones will become a smaller and smaller part of who you were. They will still serve as a reminder of how far you have come as a person and may still occasionally sadden you, but you will find the strength and courage to live a full life, in spite of them.

Faith

What is faith? Some say that it is their belief in religion and their god, while others say that it is an abstract force that helps them survive the ordeal they have been through. Let us look at faith in all its facets here.

Hope and faith are the silent whispers of courage that echo in your heart when you face abuse and betrayal. These two forces act as the light that guides you through the darkest chapters of your story. As a survivor, hope and faith are not just words—they are your lifeline, a reminder that there is a bigger story unfolding beyond the pain you have endured.

Betrayal may leave wounds that may feel impossible to heal. Your trust, when shattered, makes the world appear smaller and more threatening. In these moments, it is hope that nudges you to believe that your life is more than just the scars you carry. It tells you that you are not defined by the wrongs inflicted upon you, but by your capacity to rise, to rebuild, and to reclaim your narrative. Hope speaks to the possibility of a new beginning, a reminder that this chapter of suffering is not the end. It is the beginning of a story where healing, growth, and transformation are possible.

Faith, on the other hand, is the anchor that keeps you grounded. It is the belief in something bigger than yourself—a belief in the universe, in a higher power, or simply in the strength of the human spirit. Faith provides the assurance that, despite the pain, there is a purpose and a path to follow. It may be a difficult journey, but faith offers a glimmer of understanding, a reminder that even in the chaos, there is meaning. Through faith, you find the strength to trust in the process of healing, to let go of the fear that nothing will ever be the same again. It tells you that everything, including resilience, pride, and strength, will come when you need it most.

Resilience, a quality often underestimated, is born out of hope and faith. As a woman who has survived abuse, resilience is your superpower. It is the force that pushes you to rise every day, even when your heart feels heavy. It keeps you moving forward, step by step, as you rebuild your life. It is a quiet pride that says, "I am more than what happened to me. I am strong, I am capable, and I am worthy of a life filled with love and peace." This pride is not about ignoring the past but acknowledging the courage it took to survive and the strength it takes to heal.

Healing, however, is not linear. It is a journey that requires patience, self-compassion, and an unyielding belief that, with time, things will get better. You must allow yourself the space to grieve, to feel the hurt, and to mourn the loss of trust you once placed in your partner. But healing also means asking yourself, "What do I need to turn my story around?" This question is a powerful invitation to seek wholeness. It's an opportunity to look beyond the pain and imagine a life where you are free from fear and suffering. It's about reclaiming your power and creating a future where your voice is heard, your boundaries are respected, and your worth is recognized.

In this process, hope and faith become the threads that weave together the story or narrative of your new life. They remind you that, despite the betrayal and abuse, there is always a chance for renewal, growth, and love—both from within and from others. You believe in a bigger story that allows you to see yourself not as a victim, but as a resilient, powerful individual who can survive your pain and even turn it into your strength.

Strive to make hope and faith your constant companions as you turn the pages of your story and begin a new chapter—one you write with pride, resilience, healing, and wholeness.

Chapter 15:

Giving Love Another Chance

Chance is not a word to toss in the air.
It's a word to take in, a word to give yourself.
—Michelle Muriel

Pearl was only 17 when she met and married her first husband, a soldier. Her husband was a womanizer, but Pearl put up with it because she was too young and naive to think of an alternative course. Her husband used to bring home his girlfriends and abuse her in their presence. One time, she contracted an STI from him just before giving birth to her daughter. Considerably upset, she could only confide in her brother's wife. Generally, Pearl knew the only advice wives were given in their society was, "That is how marriage is." In her inexperience and youth, Pearl assumed she should continue to love him and remain patient for her marriage to work out. When she got pregnant again, her husband left her because he had heard rumors that the baby wasn't his, no matter how hard she pleaded with him not to leave.

A year after their baby boy was born, Pearl's husband resurfaced, and she again gave him another chance. However, his behavior remained unchanged. Pearl was so frustrated that while leaving, she spent the loan money he had borrowed as a form of revenge for all the suffering he had caused her. In 2016, she moved on to South Africa to work, leaving her children in her mother's care.

Pearl was so bitter with her experience that she hated the very ideas of romantic love, men, and marriage. The only thing that kept her spirit alive at the time was the thought of her wonderful children back at home. However, it must have been Pearl's inherent faith and goodness that opened up her heart to her colleague and now husband, a loving, generous man who never failed to encourage her whenever she felt low. In 2019, he paid her dowry as was their custom, and they became husband and wife.

Today, Pearl continues to lead a happy life with her two children and husband in South Africa. She is a successful entrepreneur who runs Pearls Cakes and Events. She describes herself as a bubbly, ever-smiling woman, who loves to empower other woman. She also compares her love life to a vanilla cake—sweet and smooth (Muguti, 2022).

Work Hard on Yourself

Experiencing betrayal is undoubtedly one of the most painful things you can go through. It shakes your sense of trust and compromises your self-esteem and self-worth. But it doesn't have to define you. You have the power to turn this pain into a moment of growth—a turning point where you build yourself up to become stronger, more resilient, and more fulfilled than ever before. This is your time to invest in yourself fully, to work on every aspect of your life, and emerge as the best version of yourself.

In the Things You Do

After betrayal, you might feel lost, disoriented, and unsure of what to do next. But one of the most powerful ways to rebuild is to focus on the things you do—your daily habits, your goals, and how you spend your time. Prioritize activities that energize and empower you. Set small, achievable goals, whether it's picking up a new hobby, finishing a book you've always wanted to read, or getting back to a fitness routine. It's not about filling up your time; it's about doing things that remind you of your strengths and passions.

Engaging in things you love allows you to reconnect with your authentic self and discover new talents and interests. Whether you choose to start painting, take up yoga, volunteer, or explore cooking, every new experience adds to your skill set and self-confidence. It's an opportunity to remind yourself of all the things you're capable of, independent of anyone else.

In Who You Are and Your Appearance

This is also a time to reconnect with who you are at your core. Betrayal can make you question your worth, but it's important to remember that what happened does not reflect your value. You are still the kind, intelligent, and strong woman you've always been, and now is your chance to fully embrace those qualities. Take time to reflect on your values—what you stand for, and what brings you joy. Journal your thoughts and use this process to attain more clarity on the kind of person you want to be and the life you want to lead.

Additionally, taking care of your physical appearance may sound a little frivolous. It isn't about pleasing others, but rather about making yourself feel good. Self-care routines, like taking care of your skin, exercising, or dressing up, can be small but significant ways to boost your self-esteem. When you look in the mirror and see yourself looking strong, confident, and put together, it reflects the strength you are building inside. Choose to look and feel your best for yourself because you deserve to feel proud of the person staring back at you.

In People You Show Up For

As you work on yourself, surround yourself with people who uplift and encourage you. Real friends and loved ones remind you of your worth when you might struggle to see it. Invest in those relationships and show up for the people who have always shown up for you. The support system you build during this time will help you navigate difficult moments, and in return, being there for them will remind you of your capacity to love, give, and connect.

At the same time, be intentional about the energy you allow into your life. You may need to distance yourself from those who don't contribute to your growth or who may drain you emotionally. You deserve people who celebrate your journey of self-improvement, not those who try to bring you down.

In Affirming Your Power

Betrayal often causes you to doubt your self-worth. But your value is not dependent on someone else's treatment of you. Remind yourself that you are deserving of love, respect, and happiness—none of these things are earned by anyone else's approval.

Rebuilding your self-esteem takes time, but it starts with small, consistent affirmations of your worth. Write down daily affirmations, list things you love about yourself, and take note of your achievements, big or small. The more you affirm your value to yourself, the less the betrayal of others will influence how you see yourself.

In Building Confidence Via Experiences

One of the most effective ways to build confidence is through action. Engaging in things you excel at will remind you of your abilities and talents, while trying new experiences pushes you out of your comfort zone and broadens your perspective. This could be anything from learning a new skill, like yoga or coding, to taking on an adventure like hiking a trail you've never explored before.

By adding to your experiences, you're not just learning new things—you're proving to yourself that you are adaptable, capable, and resilient. Every accomplishment, no matter how small, is evidence of your strength and growth. Over time, these experiences build a firm foundation of confidence that no one can shake, not even the person who betrayed you.

Betrayal may have been the catalyst, but the work you do now is entirely about you. It's about reclaiming your power, focusing on your growth, and investing in the person you see yourself becoming. You are worthy of a life filled with joy, confidence, and fulfillment—a lifestyle on your terms, independent of anyone else's actions or approval.

Remember, this is your journey, and every step you take is a testament to your strength. Believe in your ability to rebuild and redefine your life. You have everything you need within you to create a beautiful, fulfilling future.

Invite and Invoke Love Back Into Your Life

Inviting love back into your life after experiencing betrayal and heartache is a journey of healing and renewal. It requires time, patience, and a deep sense of self-care. You've been through a lot, and it's okay to acknowledge that the pain you've felt is real. Here's how you can begin to open your heart again, step by step:

Grieve

First and foremost, allow yourself to grieve. Heartbreak is a loss, and it deserves the space to be felt. You might feel anger, sadness, or even a sense of confusion and self-doubt. It's essential not to suppress these emotions or push them aside in the hopes that ignoring them will make them disappear. Instead, give yourself permission to sit with your feelings. Cry if you need to, journal your thoughts, or talk to a trusted friend. Your grief is valid, and only by moving through it can you begin to heal. Healing isn't linear, and some days might feel harder than others, but trust that each moment you allow yourself to grieve brings you one step closer to recovery.

Self-Compassion

While grieving, practice self-compassion. It's easy to be hard on yourself or feel as though you should have done something differently to prevent what happened. However, blaming yourself will only deepen the wound. Remind yourself that you did the best you could with the information and love you had at the time. Offer yourself the same kindness you would give to a friend who has been hurt. Nurture yourself through acts of self-care, whether it's taking long walks, practicing yoga, reading books that uplift your spirit, or simply resting. This stage is about reconnecting with the parts of yourself that need love and support the most. Treat yourself with the tenderness you deserve.

Identify Your Values

After the initial wave of grief has passed, you might begin to find clarity about what truly matters to you. Betrayal can shatter the foundation upon which you built your trust and values. Take some time to reflect on what you want for your life moving forward. What kind of love do you want to invite back into your life? What values are non-negotiable for you? Perhaps it's honesty, mutual respect, or shared goals. Knowing your values will serve as a guide when you decide to open your heart again, helping you choose people and situations that align with your authentic self.

Slow Trust

Once you've done some of the inner work, it's natural to feel hesitant about trusting again. Trust is something that, after being broken, needs time and careful rebuilding. It's okay to take things slowly. You don't have to let people into your inner world immediately. Instead, observe their actions over time, and notice if they consistently show up with the integrity and respect that align with your values. Allow trust to build gradually, and remember that it's not a race. There's no timeline for when you should be "over" your past or ready to trust again. Move at a pace that feels right for you.

Slow Love

Inviting love back into your life doesn't mean diving into a new relationship right away. It's about opening yourself up to the possibility of love in a slow, intentional way. Take time to reconnect with your own desires, what excites you, and what brings you joy. When you do feel ready to explore a new connection, let it unfold naturally. Don't rush into defining things or placing expectations on how things should be. Let love grow organically, with the understanding that you are a stronger, wiser version of yourself now.

Remember, your heart has been through a lot, but it also has the capacity to heal and flourish again. You deserve a love that honors your values, respects your boundaries, and nurtures your growth. Trust yourself to know when you're ready, and give yourself the grace to take each step at your own pace. You are worthy of the love you seek, and it will find you when the time is ripe.

Chapter 16:

Helping Others Find Their Voice

No one has ever become poor by giving.
−Anne Frank

Claire Conlan shares the nightmare she got sucked into around the time she was 30 years old. She had just moved back to NYC from LA after a not-so-successful stint in acting. She was also planning to support her dream of acting with the supplementary income of a yoga teacher. When she met her now-ex, she had a vague feeling he was bad news. However, his charm and seeming warmth left her dizzy. He kept praising her and showering her with so much love that she became convinced. Even her friends were fooled by the show he put on and silenced the doubts she occasionally harbored.

Claire found out the worst way possible—on the eve of her 30th birthday. While going through her partner's laptop, she stumbled upon racy emails he had been sending and receiving from his ex-girlfriend. Unlike her past relationships, this was the first time her partner deliberately seemed to keep her apart from his female friends. She was always on tenterhooks about his whereabouts and activities. Whenever she confronted him, he would turn the blame back on her, insisting she deal with her insecurities and questioning how he could live with a woman who refused to trust him.

Though Claire left, she was soon sucked back into his apologies, lies, and manipulation. She lost weight and the stress of it soon manifested in allergic reactions all over her face. She felt like an imposter teaching and preaching yoga when she felt everything but peace. Her casting director refused her a role until she got better. Her relationship was affecting every aspect of her life.

Ultimately, it was her ex's message to her friend, asking them to "take care of her because she was crazy," that opened Claire's eyes. She realized she had become this "crazy," obsessed person due to his manipulation. He had, in fact, been dating other women behind her back. Even the dog he gifted Claire was purchased with one of his other girlfriends, whom he hadn't even properly cropped out of the photo he shared with her!

Today, Claire understands that she had been in a relationship with a narcissist and a sociopath. It took her a long time to mentally free herself of that relationship, but she did. Now, she has become what she once needed—an older, wiser, friend and guide to women who are trapped in toxic relationships and grappling daily with gaslighting, lying, and manipulation on a daily basis. She can confidently say that she is a stronger, healthier, and happier woman for having experienced and shared her story (Conlan, 2024).

Setting Boundaries

We may have touched upon this subject before, but its importance is so great that we can't but emphasize it enough. Setting boundaries after betrayal and heartache is a powerful step in reclaiming your sense of self. Boundaries are the limits you establish to protect your well-being, ensuring that your energy, body, mind, and time are respected. Boundaries help you determine what you're comfortable with and allow you to create safe spaces where you feel valued. It's not only fair to set boundaries—it's necessary. People do not have a right to your inner world unless you choose to let them in.

Learning to say *no* is an essential part of boundary-setting. It can feel uncomfortable at first, especially if you're used to putting others 'needs before your own. Remember, saying no is not an act of rejection; it's an affirmation of your priorities and well-being. You have the right to refuse anything that doesn't align with your values or needs. Saying no is a powerful way to honor yourself.

Communicating your boundaries clearly is crucial. Express what you need with confidence and be prepared to repeat yourself if necessary. Not everyone will understand your boundaries immediately, and some may even test them. Consistent communication ensures your message is heard and reinforces the importance of your needs. If someone repeatedly crosses your boundaries, it's okay to establish consequences.

Establishing consequences isn't about punishing others; it's about protecting yourself. If someone disrespects your boundary, you have the right to decide what action you'll take to safeguard your well-being, whether that's stepping back from the relationship or limiting contact. The key is to follow through with the consequences you set. By doing so, you demonstrate that your boundaries are serious and non-negotiable, reinforcing your commitment to your own health and healing.

Remember, setting boundaries is an act of self-love. It's a declaration that you deserve respect, and it empowers you to build connections that honor your values and protect your heart. You are worthy of the space and safety boundaries provide.

Reclaiming Your Voice

When you've been hurt, it's common to feel silenced, as if your story doesn't matter or your feelings aren't valid. But finding your voice again is essential in reclaiming your power and moving forward.

Start by writing down your thoughts and feelings. Journaling is a powerful tool for self-discovery and release. In the privacy of your journal, you can express your pain, anger, and hopes without judgment. It's a safe space to make sense of your experiences and begin to reshape your narrative. Your story matters, and writing it down helps you take ownership of it.

Seek out people who have gone through similar experiences. You are not alone—many have faced betrayal and heartache, and connecting with those who understand your journey can be immensely validating. Sharing your story with someone who truly *gets it* can make you feel seen and heard, reminding you that your voice is important.

It's also valuable to talk with people who may not have experienced the same pain, but genuinely care for you. Trusted friends can offer fresh perspectives and empathy, helping you feel supported and understood. Even if they haven't walked in your shoes, their willingness to listen shows that your feelings are worthy of being expressed.

When you feel ready, don't hesitate to share your story with a wider audience. Speaking out—whether through writing, public speaking, or engaging in community groups—can be a powerful way to reclaim your voice. Your experience has value, and by sharing it, you can empower others while also solidifying your own sense of strength. You have the right to tell your story, and there is power in using your voice to heal, connect, and inspire.

Remember, your voice is a crucial part of who you are. It's time to reclaim it, not just for yourself, but for the countless others who need to hear your truth. You have a story worth telling, and the world is ready to listen.

Helping Others Find Their Voice

Once you've gone through pain and emerged stronger, sharing your story can be an act of courage, but it's essential to take your time. There's no rush to tell your story before you're ready; when the time comes, you'll know how to share it in a way that brings light and hope. Your journey is yours to own, and when you're prepared to open up, your narrative can become a beacon for others finding their own way.

Honesty is vital when supporting others. Be honest about your own experiences, but also be honest with others about theirs. Encourage them to speak their truth, and let them know that their emotions are valid, no matter how messy or complicated they may seem. Honesty doesn't have to be harsh; it can be paired with kindness. Let your words and actions show that you embody a safe space where they can explore their voice without judgment. Kindness and honesty can coexist beautifully. When you approach someone with both, you create a nurturing environment where they can open up and grow. Your honesty shows that you respect them enough to be real, while your kindness reassures them that they are supported and valued, no matter what.

Helping others is not only emotionally fulfilling, but also physically and mentally rejuvenating. Offering your support and guidance can bring you a renewed sense of purpose. It's a reminder that, despite your own pain, you have the strength to uplift others. This generous act can bring immense joy and healing into your own life.

Perhaps, in helping others find their voice, you'll discover a purpose you didn't realize was missing. Your experiences, though deeply painful, have the potential to be transformative—not only for you but for the countless others waiting for someone like you to show them they aren't alone. What greater testament to your healing journey can there be than using your kindness, honesty, and patience to help others reclaim their power and find their identity and voice again?

Conclusion

As we reach this final section of *He Did What? True Stories of Resilient Women Who Rose Above Betrayal and How You Can, Too,* I hope you've found inspiration and strength in the stories shared by these incredible women. Each chapter has demonstrated not only the pain and heartache they endured, but also their resilience, courage, and determination to reclaim their lives. These stories show us that betrayal and abuse, while devastating, do not define you. You have the power to rebuild and thrive, regardless of where you come from, how old you are, or what your circumstances may be.

The women in this book come from all walks of life, representing different ages, cultural backgrounds, and economic situations. Yet, despite their diverse stories, a common thread connects them: the unbreakable human spirit. They have each faced the unimaginable, and through their experiences, they have proven that healing and transformation are possible. No matter how overwhelming the pain or how deep the betrayal, you, too, have the strength within you to rise above.

One of the most powerful lessons we can take from these brave women is that healing is not a linear journey. It is messy, unpredictable, and often feels like two steps forward and one step back. But that is okay. There will be days when the weight of the past feels unbearable, and there will be days when you feel like you're moving forward with renewed hope and clarity. The important thing is to be patient with yourself and trust that you are moving in the right direction. Healing takes time, and it's essential to honor that process.

Another key aspect we came back to time and again is the importance of finding support. Many of the women featured in this book found strength in building a community—whether through friends, family, support groups, or professional help. You don't have to go through this alone, and you shouldn't. Reaching out for help is not a sign of weakness; it's an act of courage. The people who love you want to see you rise, and allowing them to support you can be a uniquely transformative experience. If you haven't yet found your community, don't give up. The right support system is out there, and connecting with others who understand your pain can make a significant difference in your healing journey.

Reclaiming your voice and setting boundaries have also emerged as powerful weapons via these women's stories. Many found their strength in learning to speak their truth, whether through journaling, therapy, or sharing their experiences with trusted individuals. Owning your story and expressing your emotions is a critical step in healing. It allows you to process the pain and move beyond it. Your voice is powerful, and it deserves to be heard.

Setting boundaries is another fundamental part of recovery. Betrayal and abuse often leave you feeling powerless and unsure of your worth. But boundaries help you reclaim that power. They are a way of saying, "I value myself enough to protect my space, my energy, and my heart." Setting boundaries may not be easy, especially if you're used to putting others first, but it's an act of self-love that helps create a safer, healthier space for you to heal and grow.

One of the most hopeful messages is that life after betrayal is not only possible—it can be full of joy, success, and fulfillment. The women featured here didn't just survive; they thrived. They pursued new careers, found new passions, and created meaningful relationships built on trust and respect. They discovered they were stronger and more capable than they had ever imagined. Your past does not have to dictate your future. You have the power to redefine your life on your terms.

As you close this book, remember you are not alone. The stories you've read are not just about other women; they are a reflection of the strength and potential within you. Healing from betrayal, abuse, or trauma is not about forgetting what happened, but rather about taking those experiences and using them as stepping stones toward a better, brighter future. You are resilient. You have the ability to transform your pain into power and create a life filled with love, peace, and fulfillment.

If you're still struggling, remember it is okay to ask for help. Therapy, support groups, and reaching out to loved ones are all ways to build your support network. Take things one day at a time, have moments of vulnerability, and allow yourself to grieve. Healing is not about perfection; it's about progress. Even the smallest steps you take will lead you closer to reclaiming your life.

Finally, I encourage you to keep your heart open to new possibilities. Love, trust, and joy are still out there for you. It's natural to feel guarded after experiencing betrayal, but you are deserving of a love that is safe, respectful, and kind. Take the lessons you've learned from your experiences and use them to build healthier, stronger connections moving forward. You have the wisdom and strength to protect your heart while still allowing it to open when the right opportunity comes.

He Did What? True Stories of Resilient Women Who Rose Above Betrayal and How You Can, Too is not just a collection of stories; it's a testament to the resilience of women everywhere. It's a reminder that no matter what you've gone through, you have the power to rise, rebuild, and create a life you love. Let these stories be a source of hope, strength, and inspiration as you continue your journey. Just like the incredible women in these pages, your story of resilience is waiting to unfold...

References

Addo. (2018, July 18). *Ashlynn's recovery story*. Addorecovery.com. https://www.addorecovery.com/betrayal-trauma/ashlynn-s-recovery-story

Alex. (2024, June 23). *This is what 30 years of emotional abuse feels like*. Betrayal Trauma Recovery. https://www.btr.org/emotional-abuse-feels-like/

Anonymous. (2010, March 19). *O magazine's true story of woman's journey to getting over infidelity*. Oprah. journey-to-getting-over-infidelity/all

Aristotle. (n.d.). *Forbes quotes: Thoughts on the business of life*. Forbes. https://www.forbes.com/quotes/642/

Balan, D. (2024). *When forgiveness can be detrimental to trauma recovery*. Psychology Today. https://www.psychologytoday.com/intl/blog/un-numb/202404/when-forgiveness-can-be-detrimental-to-trauma-recovery

Bogen, K. (2017, January 3). *Vox First Person: The 7 things I did to get over a big breakup — and why research says they work*. Vox. https://www.vox.com/first-person/2017/1/3/13938008/breakup-strategies-research

Brown, B & TED. (2011). *The power of vulnerability [Online video]*. YouTube. https://www.youtube.com/watch?v=iCvmsMzlF7o

Carter, L. K. D. (2023). *The intimacy of sisterhood*. Psychology Today. https://www.psychologytoday.com/intl/blog/inside-intimacy/202309/the-intimacy-of-sisterhood

Cheadle, L. (2023, January 26). *Episode 201: Life after betrayal with Lora Cheadle (K. Anthony, Interviewer) [Podcast Interview]*. Kate Anthony. https://kateanthony.com/podcast/life-after-betrayal-with-lora-cheadle/

Clarissa Pinkola Estes quotes. (2024). Friends of Silence. https://friendsofsilence.net/quote/author/clarissa-pinkola-estes

Conlan, C. (2024). *My heartbreak story*. Clairetheheartbreakcoach.com. https://www.clairetheheartbreakcoach.com/my-heartbreak-story

DeAngelis, T. (2002, June 1). How do mind-body interventions affect breast cancer? *Monitor on Psychology, 33*(6). https://www.apa.org/monitor/jun02/mindbody

El DeBarge quote. (2024). Quotefancy. https://quotefancy.com/quote/1601886/El-DeBarge-I-want-the-world-to-know-that-everybody-deserves-a-second-chance

Fatima Bhutto quotes. (2020). Goodreads. https://www.goodreads.com/author/quotes/55254.Fatima_Bhutto

Firestone, L. (2022, January 19). *Why is it so hard to leave a narcissist?* Psychology Today. https://www.psychologytoday.com/us/blog/compassion-matters/202201/why-is-it-so-hard-leave-narcissist

Greenberg, E. (2018, January 31). *Why is it so hard to leave the narcissist in your life?* Psychology Today. https://www.psychologytoday.com/us/blog/understanding-narcissism/201801/why-is-it-so-hard-to-leave-the-narcissist-in-your-life

Griffin, V. M. (2023, August 15). *Overcoming unthinkable betrayal and heartache: Venus Morris Griffin shares her story (V. Quigley, Interviewer) [Interview].* YouTube. https://www.youtube.com/watch?v=GjWhub9hgFw

Johnson, A. (2015, March 27). *Let go of control: How to learn the art of surrender.* Tiny Buddha. https://tinybuddha.com/blog/let-go-of-control-how-to-learn-the-art-of-surrender/

Johnson, D. (2021). *Choosing words for healing and hope in 2021.* Parkview Health. https://www.parkview.com/blog/choosing-words-for-healing-and-hope-in-2021

Kathleen. (n.d.). *Porn is abuse: Here's why — Kathleen's story (A. Blythe, Interviewer) [Interview].* Betrayal Trauma Recovery. https://www.btr.org/porn-is-abuse-heres-why/

Kingsolver, B. (2024). *A quote from The Poisonwood Bible.* Goodreads. https://www.goodreads.com/quotes/3896-every-betrayal-contains-a-perfect-moment-a-coin-stamped-heads

Leigh Bardugo quotes. (2017). Goodreads. https://www.goodreads.com/quotes/8748814-sisters-in-battle-i-am-shield-and-blade-to-you

Lindberg, S. (2018, August 31). *How to let go: 12 tips for letting go of the past.* Healthline. https://www.healthline.com/health/how-to-let-go#Tips-for-letting-go

Mason Cooley quote. (2024). Quotefancy. https://quotefancy.com/quote/1144858/Mason-Cooley-Narcissus-weeps-to-find-that-his-Image-does-not-return-his-love

Mile High Mamas. (2017, October 9). *When you meet the other woman: A strange kind of sisterhood.* Mile High Mamas. https://www.milehighmamas.com/blog/2017/10/09/when-you-meet-the-other-woman/

Mitts, C. (2023, June 8). *Anger in a relationship: Is it a red flag to have anger in your relationship?* Ipseity Counseling. https://ipseitycounselingclinic.com/2023/06/08/anger-in-a-relationship/

Muguti, P. S. (2022, February 14). *A woman's story of finding true love after heartbreak (T. Rungisa, Interviewer) [Interview].* The Weight She Carries. https://theweightshecarries.com/a-womans-story-of-finding-true-love-after-heartbreak/

Navarra, D. R. (2020, January 30). *The positive side of anger in relationships: A door to increasing intimacy*. Dr. Robert Navarra. https://drrobertnavarra.com/the-positive-side-of-anger-in-relationships-a-door-to-increasing-intimacy/

Proverbs 31:25-31 NLT. (n.d.). You Version Bible. https://www.bible.com/bible/116/PRO.31.25-31.NLT

A quote by Anne Frank. (n.d.). Goodreads. https://www.goodreads.com/quotes/81804-no-one-has-ever-become-poor-by-giving

A quote by Elizabeth Gilbert. (2024). Goodreads. https://www.goodreads.com/quotes/244961-someday-you-re-gonna-look-back-on-this-moment-of-your

A quote by Friedrich Nietzsche. (n.d.). Goodreads. https://www.goodreads.com/quotes/11864-i-m-not-upset-that-you-lied-to-me-i-m-upset

A quote by Margaret Thatcher. (n.d.). Goodreads. https://www.goodreads.com/quotes/63419-in-politics-if-you-want-anything-said-ask-a-man

A quote by Michelle Muriel. (2020). Goodreads. https://www.goodreads.com/quotes/9927413-chance-is-not-a-word-to-toss-in-the-air

A quote by Shannon L. Alder. (2024). Goodreads. https://www.goodreads.com/quotes/795135-there-comes-a-time-in-your-life-when-you-have

Quoteresearch. (2017, August 19). *Resentment is like taking poison and waiting for the other person to die.* Quote Investigator. https://quoteinvestigator.com/2017/08/19/resentment/

Ratliff, J. (2016, December 28). *To anyone who struggles with "letting go."* Medium. https://medium.com/personal-growth/to-anyone-who-struggles-with-letting-go-ed5bf12fb1e6

Rind, V. (2016, April 21). *My husband's financial infidelity.* Next Avenue. https://www.nextavenue.org/rebounding-from-my-husbands-financial-infidelity/

Sherman, B. (1992, November 29). *Leading a double life is more common than many suspect.* Los Angeles Times. https://www.latimes.com/archives/la-xpm-1992-11-29-vw-2591-story.html

Sherrilyn Kenyon quotes. (2024). Goodreads. https://www.goodreads.com/quotes/375040-everyone-suffers-at-least-one-bad-betrayal-in-their-lifetime

Silva, S. (2023, May 19). *My spectacular betrayal.* The New York Times. https://www.nytimes.com/2023/05/19/style/modern-love-affair-therapy-spectacular-betrayal.html

Smith, K. (2022, November 18). *How to control anger and frustration in a relationship.* HealthCentral. https://www.healthcentral.com/sex-and-relationships/control-anger-frustration-relationship

Starting life over at 52: How to overcome heartbreak and betrayal. (2024, February 19). *Time with Natalie.* YouTube. https://www.youtube.com/watch?v=9GCXyDa25ZY

S. Timothy Brown. (2019, July 15). *Betrayal trauma in action: Daisy's story.* The Modern Mr. And Mrs. https://www.themodernmrandmrs.com/2019/07/15/betrayal-trauma-in-action-daisys-story/

Street, E. (Ed.). (2024, September 9). *Cheating statistics 2024: Do men really cheat more than women?* Techopedia. https://www.techopedia.com/statistics/cheating-statistics

Szczepanski, S. (2024, June 4). *How one woman rebuilt her life after betrayal and deception (R. Story, Interviewer) [Interview].* YouTube. https://www.youtube.com/watch?v=pzuuJtTcnw8

Szczepanski, S. (2023, December 6). *Episode 158: Unlocking Love after Catfish Deception (H. Bee, Interviewer) [Podcast Interview].* Your Divorce Planner. https://shows.acast.com/divorce-comeback-coach/episodes/158-unlocking-love-after-catfish-deception

You did what you knew how to do, and when you knew better, you did better. (2022, November 30). Quoteinvestigator. https://quoteinvestigator.com/2022/11/30/did-better/

Vaughan, P. (2009). *The Monogamy Myth.* Harper Collins.

Veronica Roth quotes. (2024). Goodreads. https://www.goodreads.com/quotes/553786-i-could-never-hurt-him-enough-to-make-his-betrayal

Vi, & Schrader, C. (2022, March 30). *Participant story: Overcoming abuse and betrayal.* The Sunflower Effect. https://www.makingmoves.net/inspiring-story-overcoming-abuse-betrayal/

Weintraub, A. (2023, July 10). *"Betrayal": Woman unravels husband's double life after he's charged with sexually assaulting student.* ABC News. https://abcnews.go.com/US/betrayal-woman-unravels-husbands-double-life-after-charged/story?id=100539713%20https://1girlrevolution.com/jeniferfaison/

Why is leaving a narcissist so hard? (2022, December 21). Nussbaum Law. https://nussbaumlaw.ca/leaving-a-narcissist/

www.ingramcontent.com/pod-product-compliance
Lightning Source LLC
Chambersburg PA
CBHW052137270326
41930CB00012B/2922